A Thought for Today

Rance Williams

Sunrise comes to the Golan Heights
and the Sea of Galilee, Israel.

*"The people who sat in darkness
have seen a great light, and
upon those who sat in the
region and shadow of death,
light has dawned."*

Matthew 4:16

Photo by the author
May, 2010

A Thought for Today

Printed in the United States of America

Library of Congress Number: 2017902296
International Standard Book Number: 978-1-60126-527-2

Masthof Press
219 Mill Road | Morgantown, PA 19543
www.masthof.com

This book is a gift.

From the **beginning,** when the idea was born to **share** the many quotes and sayings from my Bible study collection, it was **never** my intent to publish for profit. If you find something in these pages that **blesses, challenges, or even jabs** you a little, that will be payment enough.

Should you wish to **send a copy** to someone you think might **benefit** from its content, all I ask is the amount to cover the cost of mailing. **Your feedback** is welcomed. Send me an email at **rancefw@msn.com.** *Thank you.*

Rance Williams

5109 Sandy Shore Ave.

Sarasota, Florida 34242

"The grass withers, the flower fades,
But the word of our God stands forever".

Isaiah 40:8

DEDICATION

This book is dedicated to my beloved sister,
friend, spiritual model and
family matriarch:

LEILA WILLIAMS CLYMER

July 2, 1936 - March 16, 2015

"Charm is deceitful and beauty is passing,
But a woman who fears the Lord, she shall be praised."

Proverbs 31:30

TABLE OF CONTENTS

PREFACE

All through the **labor of love** that went into the work of assembling, sorting, and editing *A Thought for Today*, my **heart's desire** was twofold:

1. To put a book into the hands of Christians that would **bless** as well as **awaken** them to what is currently taking place in what we commonly refer to as **"the church."**
2. Strengthen these same believers for the **current** as well as **future battles** that are sure to come as this world slides deeper and deeper **into secularism** and **away from God.**

Now, the question is: Can **a book** accomplish these goals? Many a person has picked up a book with no more intention than to **pass some time away** or simply **learn** what someone has to say about a particular subject. Sometimes that person has come away with **new** convictions and new opinions, **because they read a book.**

So, with that thought in mind, allow me to **share with you** what **A. W. Tozer** wrote concerning the reading of **Christian based books:**

"Perhaps a word of warning would not be amiss here: It is that we beware the common habit of putting confidence in books**, as such.** It takes a determined effort of the mind to break free from the error of making books and teachers **ends in themselves.**

The **worst** thing a book can do for a Christian is to leave him with the impression that he has received from it **anything**

really good; the best it can do is to **point the way** to the Good he is seeking. The function of a good book is to **stand like a signpost** directing the reader towards the **Truth** and the **Life.** That book serves best which early makes itself **unnecessary,** just as a signpost serves best after it is **forgotten**, after the traveler has **arrived safely** at his desired haven. The work of a good book is **to incite** the reader to **moral** action, to **turn** his eyes toward God and **urge** him forward. Beyond that it cannot go."

I honestly feel that within these pages are **many signposts.** I pray that they lead you to a place that **feeds and strengthens** your inner soul.

INTRODUCTION

This book is the result of years of Bible study and preparation for Sunday school lessons that I taught. As a teacher, I often began my lesson with **"A Thought for Today"**, something someone had said or written that was **thought provoking, challenging, or reflective** about the topic for that day. The **primary provider** of material for my lessons was the **Holy Spirit**. Hours of research, study, and quiet time allowed my soul to reach out for God's **direction, wisdom, and help**. Those of you who have taught **know** exactly what I mean. When a deadline looms, **only** the Spirit of God can help.

I also leaned heavily on great writers, men of God, who helped me understand some difficult passages of scripture. Their commentary often brought the lessons alive. Some of these men were **A. W. Tozer,** Warren **Wiersbe,** William **MacDonald,** Charles **Swindoll**, and even Matthew **Henry (1662–1714)** from long ago.

Over time, some of my students gave me quotes or thoughts they had saved. This gave me the **assurance and confidence** that people had an interest in what I was doing.

Within this book, if I **borrowed** a quote, I have tried to reference that person. Sometimes, however, I did not record the name because I never **intended** to write a book. So, if you **recognize** something that I quoted (or misquoted) and did not mention the author, please accept my sincere **apology.**

Please note that the use of ***bold print*** throughout this book was added by ***the author*** for the purpose of emphasis. In addition, all scripture quoted is from the ***New King James Version*** of the Bible unless otherwise noted.

To those of you who take the time to browse through this collection, thank you. The content was **primarily written** for Christians. It is my hope that those readers will see something that will make them **stop, think, and meditate.** If you are **not** a believer or follower of Christ, I have a quiet **suggestion.** Please start in the back of this book where there is a short, simple text called **The Plan of Salvation.** Nothing is as important to you as that page. Please read it first, **follow the steps,** and then **life itself,** as well as this book, will really **make sense** to you.

Blessings,

Rance Williams

PART ONE
The Bible

CHAPTER ONE

The Bible–God's Holy Word

Personally, I love the Bible, always have, and always will. Now, that doesn't mean I have spent a lifetime studying and following its truths because I haven't. However, the Bible always has been the **life vest** I reached for whenever the **storms of life** came crashing down around me.

As a child, I remember my dad reading the great stories of **David, Jonah, and Jesus**. We were not a religious family, though my folks did take us to church, but we were taught **respect and reverence** for God's Book. It was not to be ridiculed.

As an adult, though mostly apart from its influence, I still remembered where my escape lay when caught in **my own web or desert**. Only within the last 20 years have I seriously returned to its message and dedicated its message to my heart. The beautiful thing is that after studying each and every book individually, from Genesis to Revelation, there is something **new and fresh** for my soul every day.

His story (history) is all there. Within its pages, God reveals **Himself** and His **purpose** for man through a loving invitation for fellowship and forgiveness of sin or, as in my case, rebellion. His **love, mercy**, and **desire** for man to spend eternity with Him is clear and simple. It's **His invitation**, and it's **our choice.**

So, within these selections, I hope you find a thought or be challenged by something that will stir your soul and give you a **new and fresh appreciation** for the Bible and the things of God.

God is Not Mocked

Allow me to start with this intriguing story about **French philosopher, Voltaire**. He boasted while alive that **within 100 years of his death** the Bible would disappear from the face of the earth. Well, we all know the truth of that prediction, but here **is the irony**:

*Within **50 years** of his death, the Geneva Bible Society had moved into his former home and used **his presses to print thousands of Bibles.***

Simple Truths from a Simple Man

*"I believe that the Bible is **the best gift** that God has given to man…But for this Book we could not know **right from wrong…**Take all you can of this Book **upon reason,** and the balance on **faith,** and you will live and die a **happier man."***
Abraham Lincoln

Three Keys to Bible Study

When you open your Bible to study God's Word, here is a good prayer to whisper to yourself **before you start**:

*"Lord, when I read Your Word, may my **eyes** see it, my **mind** read it, and my **heart** retain it."*

Present and Future Thought

Is there **anything** to calm our troubled spirits with today's headlines? Yes, remember:

*"In God's Word we **constantly see** that present **assurance** will lead to future **deliverance."***
Unknown

The Alpha and Omega

Matthew Henry made this comment regarding **Psalm 110:**

*"For as the New Testament **explains** the Old, so the Old Testament **confirms** the New, and Jesus Christ is **the Alpha and Omega** of both."*

The Bible and the Test of Time

Today **unbelievers** and outright **enemies** of God are going out of their way to **mock and discredit** the Bible any way they can. The scriptures have **been through** this battle before. So the answer to **its critics** is this:

*"God's threats may be **vilified**, but cannot be **nullified** by the unbelief of man."*   **Unknown**

The Bible and Prophecy

One of the truths that **confirms** the accuracy and faith in the Bible is its **prophecy** and **predicting the future**. Keep in mind that prophecy's **main purpose** is to:

*"Provide **encouragement**, along with **correction and warnings**, and to **communicate God's message** to all people."*   **Unknown**

Interesting Fact and Statement

The exact center of the Bible is **Psalms 118:8** and the verse reads as follows, "It is **better** to trust in the **Lord**, than **put confidence in man.**" So, no matter which **direction** you choose to go, to Old Testament faith or New Testament grace, the message will not change.

Two Good Assets

When we **ponder** what it takes to get through this crazy world, here's a good start:

*"With the **Word of God in our hands** and the **Spirit of God in our hearts,** we have all that we need **for instruction** in the truth of God."* **Unknown**

The Sinless Nature of Christ

Listen to those who **walked** with Jesus and what **they** say about the Bible doctrine of the **sinless life** of Christ:

Peter *tells us, "He **did** no sin"; **Paul** said, "He **knew** no sin"; and **John**, who we know from scripture had a close relationship with Christ said, "In Him **is** no sin."*

More Bible Doctrine –Mercy and Justice

Mercy and justice are part of the **foundation of God's character** and must be kept in balance. How? Listen…

*"**Excess mercy** excuses wrong doing, however, **justice** cannot forget mercy. But **mercy** without **justice leaves people in their sin** and justice without mercy will **drive people away** from God."* **Unknown**

Therefore, it is **proper** to turn to **Hosea 12:6** where we read, *"Observe mercy **and** justice, and wait on your God **continually."***

Gathering Fruit

Here is a stirring **visual picture** from the great theological reformer, **Martin Luther:**

> *"I study my Bible as I **gather apples**. **First, I shake** the whole tree that the **ripest** might fall. Then I shake **each limb**, and when I have shaken each limb, I shake **each branch** and every **twig**. Then I look **under every leaf.**"* Now **that** my brother **is gleaning** God's Word....

No Stamps Required

Not too long ago people wrote **nice long letters** to each other. Think about what our heavenly Father wrote to us in this thought:

> *"**The Bible** is a letter God has sent to us; **prayer** is a letter we send to Him."*   **Matthew Henry**

The Bible Russian Style

Although we know there is a **vast underground church** in Russia, many Christians must **stay hidden.** If you're wondering **why,** this is how the **Russian dictionary** describes the Bible:

> *"A collection of **fantastic legends** without scientific support. It is full of **dark hints,** historical **mistakes and contradictions.** It serves as a factor **for gaining power** and subjugating **unknowing nations.**"*

New Day, New Light

Warren Wiersbe wrote this gem concerning the Bible:

*"One of the **beautiful things** about the inspired Word of God is its **constant freshness**. No matter **how often** we read it, there is always **something new** to learn or **something familiar** to see in **a new light**."*

The Bible under Attack

The Bible is being **attacked i**n many aspects of American life. Although, in the past, we have written **thousands** upon thousands of laws to support **the 10 Commandments**, man still rejects his only **dependable source of truth** about God, man, sin, salvation, and future events. In these days of rapidly **changing ideas**, **events, and situations**, the unchanging Word of God is our only **dependable light and unshakable foundation**.

*Keep in mind what **Jesus said,** "Heaven and earth will pass away, but **my words** will never pass away."*

Matthew 24:35

The Bible Believing Remnant

As a **follow up** to the attack thought, God has always had **His remnant** of believers. It was true in the **days of Isaiah**, when God said that **in spite of** the sins in Israel, He still had *"seven thousand whose **knee had not bowed** to Baal,"* and it is still true today.

The **hope of America** lies with the people who comprise **God's** present day remnant.

Entertainment or Encouragement?

Many people, **even Christians** at times, read about **Bible prophecy** with skepticism and smiles. But someone had a better explanation:

> *"Prophecy should not be treated as entertainment for the **curious**, but encouragement for the **serious**."*

The Jews and the Bible

You know from reading God's Word that **the Jews** are indeed God's **special treasure and heritage**. Think about this:

> *"To Israel, He gave **His Laws**, His **covenants**, the **Temple** and the **priesthood**, a **special land**, and the **promise** that they would bless the whole world. And best of all **from Israel came the Bible and the gift of the Savior.**"*
>
> **Unknown**

Serious Bible Study

How serious are you about Bible Study?

Andrew Murray says we should have, *"A readiness to **believe** every promise, to **obey** every command, and stand **perfect** and **complete** in all the will of God. That is the only **true** spirit of Bible study."*

The Bible's Definition of Rest

*The Bible speaks of man's **rest** and **God's rest** in different ways:*

*First, it is mentioned as **God's rest** after the 6th day. It wasn't rest from His toil, but **in His satisfaction.***

*Canaan was to be a **land of rest** for Israel, but many failed to reach it because of sin.*

*Believers enjoy **the rest of conscience** knowing Christ's work paid the price for their sin.*

Christians taking Jesus' yoke will always find rest for their souls.

*And finally, believers look forward to **eternal rest** in glory in our Father's house.* **Unknown**

The Bible Always Tells the Truth

Sometimes the Bible seems **too open** and recounts stories and events that **shock us** about people we thought could do no wrong. This proves that even they **had skeletons** in the closet.

American columnist **Russell Baker** said, *"The **biographer's** problem is that he never knows **enough**. The **autobiographer's** problem is that he knows **too much.**"*

But when God writes a story in His Word, He knows **everything about everybody** and always tells the truth **for our own good**.

The Bible Truth about Israel's King

There is **every evidence** in the Pentateuch that God planned **someday** to give Israel a king. Israel's sin wasn't **in asking,** it was **insisting** God do it now. The Lord **had a king in mind, David,** the son of Jesse, but **the time wasn't right** so the Lord **gave them Saul** who was a disaster. Which makes me think-

> *"Sometimes **the greatest judgment** God can give us is to let us **have our own way."***   **Unknown**

Good Reasons to Study Our Bibles

Let's be completely honest: **at times** we neglect to even open God's Word. We have all types **of reasons, excuses, or attitudes.** Keep this thought in mind when it happens:

> *"The Word in the **hand** is fine; the Word in the **head** is better; but the Word in the **heart** is what transforms us and matures us in Christ."*   **Unknown**

The Bible, Jesus, and Creation

When you **clearly** see God in creation, **you know** the story came from **the Bible.** With the **same Bible** in hand, you can't help but **see Jesus as the Creator (John 1:1-3).** Look at it this way:

> *"He is seen in **the vine** (John 15), **the sun** (John 18:12), **the stars** (Num. 24:17), **the lambs** (John 1:29), **the apple trees and lilies** (Song 2:3, 16), **the seed planted in the ground** (John 12:23-24), and **the bread on the table** (John 6:35)."*   **Warren Wiersbe**

Is Your Bible a Book of Literature or a Book of Experience?

Many people say they have their Bible and need nothing more. But, it is one thing to **believe** the Bible but something else altogether to **allow** the Bible, through the Holy Spirit to **input and change lives.**

*"Likewise, it is one thing to **read** about the new birth and quite another to **experience** the birth from above. You can also **read** about the infilling of the Holy Spirit and **believe** it because it is in the Bible but it is another thing to **feel** the radical change that comes with the Holy Spirit **filling experience.**"*   **Unknown**

Watch the Translators

A popular Bible translation written for a major denomination has **dropped** the "O" and "Oh" from their text.

In **my humble opinion,** that was a **sad decision.** Quite honestly, it led me to **reject that Bible translation** and using it in my adult Sunday school lessons. Why? Because I believe it was **in the original** writings, as often used **by David in the Psalms.** We Christians should **be careful** lest we lose the "Oh" **from our** hearts.

*I agree with **A. W. Tozer** for he wrote: **"O",** that simple exclamation, becomes **more eloquent than any great oratory** to the heart of God when we drop to our knees and **cry out to Him** in reverent fear and worship, **"O Father who art in heaven, please hear my prayer..."***

CHAPTER TWO

Troubling Days and Bible Warnings

There is an old **African-American** spiritual called *"Nobody Knows the Trouble I've Seen."* In fact the first line ends, *"nobody knows **but Jesus,** "* and isn't that the truth? Troubling days are **not new** and the warnings from scripture are as old as the Word itself. So, what **is so different about today?** Primarily, in my opinion, it has to do with the obvious **spiritual decay** of our churches. As I write this I am in my seventies, and, **in my lifetime,** especially the last ten years, I have seen some dramatic changes. For example, large, main stream denominations that once stood solidly upon **the Word of God** now **embrace** same sex marriage and the ceremony may well be conducted **by** a fellow gay who stands in the pulpit. As a strong voice **against** this sinful practice as described by Paul in the Book of Romans, I foresee the day when faithful Bible teachers could be charged with **hate crimes** for sticking to their convictions opposing this volatile issue. We must win the lost to Christ, including those practicing these sins, but we cannot remove the Bible as our authority for the New Testament church.

That is just **the tip** of the preverbal iceberg. Churches that once stood upon the truths of the Bible now compromise **in the message, music, and methods**. They will do whatever it takes to meet the budget, appease members with the "new message" of the **social gospel** instead of the **cross** and deal with the older congregation members who complain with nods and smiles. Brethren, I believe we **are reaping the whirlwinds** of the rebellious sixties when society in general and churches in particular refused to **stand up** to the hi-jacking of our schools, universities and seminaries by false teachers and nonbelieving wolves in sheep's clothing. I truly believe it is all connected to end times prophecy as the Bible warns in Daniel, Revelation, and from the lips of Christ Himself in Matthew, Chapter 24.

The following is a collection of **thoughts and warnings** from authors, theologians, and preachers (past and current) who **know** and **see** what is happening. Most look back at what scriptures warned us **could** happen, what we can **learn,** and how to **hold the line** against the current forces of evil in our churches and society.

It's Important Where You Look

It seems like wherever we look in the world these days, it's gloomy. Even in the mirror, the evidence of advancing age and wrinkles depress. Here's a better idea to start your day–

*"Look at **yourself** and you'll be **depressed,** look at circumstances and you'll be **distressed,** look at **the Lord** and you'll be **blessed.**"*

Unknown

Decisions, Decisions, Decisions

Often choices, especially **critical** decisions, determine what the future holds. This is true in **our** daily lives and especially true in the life of **churches and its pastors.** Consider this thought:

*"Decisions based on **opinions** may be considered, but decisions based on **convictions** must stand unless those convictions are changed. Otherwise, **decisions become indecisions,** and the leader who ought to be a **guide post** becomes a **weather vane, blown asunder by every false wind of doctrine."*   **Unknown**

Deliverance from trouble.

Psalm 50:15 *"Call upon me in the day of trouble; and I shall deliver you, and you shall glorify me."*

Have you ever known **genuine trouble**? **When?** The Bible says that when the promised **judgment trouble** comes, it shall be as man has **never seen**. In this age we have a soft **life,** a soft **church**, and a soft **sense of trouble.** God's **judgment** will be beyond anything what the world has ever seen, heard, or read. God's **deliverance** will be the **only** true deliverance. The Lord has promised...*"I shall deliver you"*...you, being **true believers** in His name. We who are **spared** from the wrath of The Lamb shall glorify Him, because when **we see** what He has delivered us **from,** no other form of thanks **shall be appropriate**, so great will be our thanksgivings.

Bloodless Christians

Christians today have **no idea** what our forefathers had to endure **to stand** for the faith. We live in a safe America, away from the threat of religious fanatics, those who would slay us simply because we name the name of Christ. **Charles Swindoll** put it very well when he wrote–

"Many Christians are **satisfied** with the benefits of their lives in which there **is no "shedding of blood."** They **give away** what they can easily spare. They engage in **sacrifice** as long as it does not involve **life,** are prominent at all **triumphant entries,** willing to buy colorful **banners** and **palm branches,** but when the "hurrahs" and "hosannas" change to **threats,** and **Calvary** comes into sight, they **steal away** into **safe** seclusion."

The Unreachable

We have **all** met someone in our lives who would **not get saved** no matter what we said or showed them **about their condition**. I found this **great explanation** some time ago:

Matthew Henry asks: *"If people will not be awakened by the greatest of things, nor allured by the sweetest of things, nor startled by the most terrible of things, nor see the plainest of things, nor listen to the voice of scripture, reason, experience, providence, conscience, or interest–what more can be done? There is none as blind as those who will not see."*

Why We Should Not Love the World

We are **plainly** warned in scripture **not** to love the world. Why? *"Because as the devil is opposed to Christ, and the flesh is hostile to the Spirit, so the world is antagonistic towards the Father."*   **Unknown**

The Christian, His Music, and the World

Recently someone told me that when they **entered their church** for worship, being **older**, they were handed a set of **ear plugs**. "What are **these for?**" he asked. He was told that **the music** was going to get "really **cranked up** today." They are now at **another church**, which is **understandable** with those of us who **still prefer** the old **songs of Zion**. Which leads to this thought:

> What **James 1:27,** ("...keep oneself unspotted from the world"), **and 1 John 2:15,** ("...do not love the world or the things of the world"), the question today of **"Christian Rock Music:"** is its tone meant to **praise** God the same as the great old hymn writers or the **music of the Psalms?** I think **not** and **personally** believe it is another **Laodicea compromise.**

Man and His Money

The **great god money** has been winning many **converts**. This fact, sad to say, is **as old as scripture** because Jesus Himself said, "you **cannot** serve God **and** mammon" (**Matt. 6:24.**) Here is another thoughtful opinion from the pen of **Warren Wiersbe–**

> "What **faith** in the Lord does for the **Christian**, money does for many **unbelievers.** They make it their god; they **love** it, **make sacrifices** for it, and think it will **save them.** Their minds are filled with **thoughts** of it, they **guard** it, their lives are **controlled** by it, and it gives them a **great sense** of **security."**

Past and Present Mistakes

It is **heartbreaking** to see what is happening to this great land of ours. If you really **study your Bible** you will see we are on the **same slippery slope** as ancient Israel. Check this out...

Philosopher **George Santayana** wrote: *"Those who* **cannot** *remember the past* **are condemned** *to* **repeat** *it."*

While we don't **live** in the past, we must **learn** from the past or we'll commit the **same mistakes**, the same **sins** against God as outlined in the Old and New Testaments. Time after time, **Israel** forgot God's mercies and **ignored** His Commandments. The Apostle **Paul** often had to **warn** the **early churches** of their straying into sin. Now it is **America's** time. Will we **learn** from the past or will we continue to take God out of our **schools, society, and lives?**

God Judges Nations

More on the same thought, just another great **example** and **warning** from God:

William MacDonald, commenting on **Ezekiel Chapter 7** said: *"**Any nation** that **rejects** the knowledge of God **loses its moral fiber** and has no means of support when **trouble comes.** For example; when God **allowed Judah** to fall into **exile,** it was **because** the king, the princes, the priests, the elders and **even the common people** totally failed and forgot God."*

What a **solemn indictment**: the **only thing** left was **judgment.**

New Ideas Needed?

In order to meet **outlandish budgets**, churches are turning to **anything** that will fill the pews. **Bingo** has replaced the Bible, **social dinners** instead of training disciples, and **drums** in place of divine, reverent silence.

Is that the kind of church the **Apostle Paul** founded? Of course not. He demanded holy worship and strong leaders for the flocks. So think about this **thought for today:**

*"In this church age of **constant change**, the Lord is **not** looking for **new** methods and programs; God is always **looking for that someone** to rightly stand for His Word. The **way and direction** of Christ's church demands **true soldiers** of the cross."* **Unknown**

Attention Christ Deniers

In **2 Timothy 2:13,** Paul is referring to Jesus when he wrote, *"He cannot deny Himself."* What did Paul **mean** by that? Paul was trying to warn really cold hard sinners…

*"That fact should be a **sobering thought** to permanent, habitual **Christ deniers.** Why? Because Christ is just **as faithful** in His **threatening** as He is in His **promises.** At the **judgment** it will be **too late** to rescind **anything** they said or did and **grace and mercy** will be **null and void."***

Unknown

No Shame in Sin

I remember as a young boy sitting around with the family watching **early TV.** The language was plain, the stories clean, and excess violence and smut were taboo. These days, TV for me is Jeopardy and sports. However, I do see enough of **just the commercials** to know that **anything goes,** and I mean **anything.** So this thought was **perfect** for what I think about American entertainment:

*"Both the Old and New Testaments give us **examples** of men who were **ashamed** of their sin: **Ezra** tore his garment and was **too ashamed** to even look towards heaven, and **the publican** in **Jesus' example** simply smote his breast. However, **America** has taken sin to a new level. When **a nation** turns **sin into entertainment** and **laughs** at what ought to make **us blush** and **cry out to God**, we are in desperate **need of revival."**   **Warren Wiersbe**

Solid Foundations but Broken Walls

The story of **Nehemiah** returning to Jerusalem and taking the **night inspection ride** on the donkey (Neh. 2:12-15), then **mobilizing** the people, and finally **leading them** in **prayer** is inspiring and one of **my favorite Bible stories**. Here's a great thought regarding those events:

*"**Nehemiah's workers** recycled all the old **solid rocks** as they **rebuilt** the walls around Jerusalem. **No new** materials were needed because the "**ruined blocks and masonry**" were **still there** in the **old foundations.***

*Today, **the wall of the church** is falling due to **neglect, scandal, and poor leadership**. But the **foundation is still there** in the Word of God and **no new materials** are needed. When the church is "**spoiled**," rebuilding is not by inventing **new clever ways** but by **going back** to the old truths that made the church great in **ages past**. These **truths** lie like rocks **in the dust**, waiting for some burdened Nehemiah to **uncover them and rebuild the wall**."*

Warren Wiersbe

Methods and Principals

Change is **not bad**. Regarding change in **the church**, this can be accomplished **as long as** we stick to the Word of God. Here's a little reminder:

*"**Methods** are many, **principals** are few,*

*Methods always **change**, principals never do."*

Unknown

Worldly Methods

As long as we are talking about methods, here is a good **point from Warren Wiersbe** that is all too common today in some churches because of **social pressures** they cannot handle. Listen:

*"Whenever **leadership** in a church decays **spiritually**, that church becomes **more like** the world and **uses** the world's **methods and resources** to do God's work."*

Church Building

Certainly the church **is more** than a building. And like its **members,** it too must be strong to withstand the **winds of change** and the **enemies** of God. So what's the answer?

*"We don't build the local church on **clever human ideas** or by **imitating the world**; we build it by **teaching** and **obeying** the precious truths of the Word of God."*
                                                              Warren Wiersbe

Changing Hearts Verses Making Laws

In the **aftermath** of the terrible mass shootings at the school in **Newtown, Conn.** there was much discussion in our Bible Study class **about how** this could have been **prevented.**

While **Christians** should do everything they can to **alleviate suffering** and make this a safer world, **especially for children,** *our hope is **not** in **laws, political alliances, or moral crusades.*** Our **hope** is in the **Lord.** People's **hearts** need to be changed by the grace of God, then many of our social ills will be easier to deal with.

Outside the Camp

In **Exodus Chapter 33: 1-11,** soon after the Exodus began, God became very **disenchanted** with the children of Israel so He had Moses **move his tent** outside the camp.

"**You are a stiff-necked people**," God said and threatened to **destroy** all of them. Only when the people had removed all their **jewelry** and **humbled** themselves did Moses **return** to the camp. Here is something to think about–

*"Our camp, America, is **polluted**. What **the Bible calls sin and abomination** we now **call** "**love**" and allow "**marriage**" between the **same sexes**. **How long** will God remain silent before **our camp is purged?**"* **Unknown**

Moral Idiots

*"There is **ground for declaring** that modern man has become a **moral idiot**,"* so declared Dr. **Richard Weaver** in **1948.**

Called a **profound diagnosis** of the sickness of our culture, his **simple message** then was that if you do not live **according to the truth**, you must suffer the **consequences.** Today's society not only **rejects** the truth **and** the consequences but they **believe in neither.** But **God's Word** is simple: *"Be **sure** your sins will **find you out.**"*

Unholy Churches

Is there **any doubt** in your mind that today we have buildings called "churches," that are anything but because of their dead message? Is this **a new present day danger** in Christianity? Listen to what **Charles H. Spurgeon** wrote in **1861**:

*"An unholy church. It has **no use** to the world, nor any **esteem** among men. It is an **abomination, hell's laughter, and heaven's abhorrence**. And the **larger** the church, the more **influential**, the worse **nuisance** does it become when it becomes **dead and unholy**. The worse **evils** which have come upon the world, have been **brought upon her** by an unholy church."*

What would **Spurgeon say** if he were alive today?

Strange Fire

When **Nadab and Abihu,** the two eldest **sons of Aaron** were struck dead in the **very area** of The Holy of Holies, it showed that with great **privilege** comes great **responsibility**. God had given Moses and Aaron **specific instructions** concerning how the various aspects of atonement were to be accomplished. However, in spite of God's warnings, **Nadab and Abihu** took things upon themselves and tried to do things **their way.** They attempted to use **their own fire** instead of that **demanded by God**. Their **disregard** became a never ending lesson of **disobedience, pride, self-will, and clerical abuse.**

Interesting, but do you know what Nadab's Hebrew name means? "Liberal."

Entertaining the Masses

How far have we moved **away** from the Bible when it comes to the entertainment business?

> *"Think about it; the **very sins** that God condemns–**murder, deceit, immorality, violence, greed,** and **blasphemy** are the very things that **entertain people** every day. Whether on TV, in books, movies, or the internet, if we were to **take the violence and vice out** of entertainment, people would **not pay** to see it."*   **Unknown**

Formula for a Great Nation

In **Deuteronomy Chapter 4: 5-9** Moses outlines the **principles for "a great nation".**

Actually, the **basics** are simple: Moses said, *"Use **wisdom, understanding, and diligence towards God** and **teach them to your children and grandchildren."***

My concern **today** is that, unless there is a turning back to God, our **grandchildren** will never know the America that we enjoyed; God fearing, blessed, and the light of the world.

Religious Fast Food

In **Judges Chapter 9**, not long after Israel **moved into** the Promised Land they became lax and did not drive out **the pagans** as God had commanded. Perhaps they stopped being **led by** the priests and became **less interested** in their covenant with God, and their **desires** went from a **stable** diet to **fast food,** so to speak. Someone said, and I happen to agree–

> *"Today we have **religious fast food** in our churches. People do not even have **to chew** on the **meat,** just fill up **on dessert** every Sunday."*

Unusual Judgment

In the Book of Judges, when **Israel** abandoned God, He did something highly unusual: **He abandoned them.**

Paul wrote something **similar** to the **Romans.** When the peoples **sins** became evil and vile to the point of **dishonoring** their own bodies, *"God gave them over"* to do those things which are not fitting. Is this not what we **are seeing in staggering numbers** in these **end times?**

Putting Out the Fleece

Gideon, when called by God **to lead Israel,** felt totally incompetent, lacking both **courage and faith.** God saw him **differently. Gideon obeyed the Lord** and tore down **his father's** altar **to Baal,** and God even gave him **a new name–** Jerubbaal– "let Baal plea."

*However, Gideon still **tested God twice** with **dry** fleece and **damp** mornings. The Lord gave him **a pass** to **strengthen his faith,** as He **sometimes** will do for us, but we **cannot continue** in that juvenile level forever.*

*The church cannot either. Sometimes **tough decisions** are necessary from the pastor and leaders, and must be made, **instead of** "putting out the fleece" to **see** what **works** with the congregation.*

Ahaz and the New Altar

Judah's godless king Ahaz not only bowed down to **the Assyrians** in fear, but even put **their new pagan altar** in the temple **in place of God's altar.**

Warren Wiersbc comments that *"this is what **the church** is doing today, **refitting itself** with **man's ideas** to make it **more comfortable** and **entertainment** has replaced **worship.**"*

The Price of Worship

In Psalm 5:7, David approaches God in prayer **with fear and reverence**. Many worship services today are anything but reverent. Someone commented:

*"Our worship should **never** be in such a **light spirit** that it approaches **cuteness and flippancy,** a time of merriment and nothing but a time of laughter."*

Today's Hostile World

In this year, **2015,** all you have to do is page through the morning paper **to see** that many **Christians in foreign lands** are in great danger, such as those in the countries where ISIS has a foothold. Someone made this observation-

*"Sadly, in America, we are **not here to fight** but to **frolic.** Born again followers need to **reexamine** their **spiritual philosophy** in the light of **the Bible.** We **cannot** be neutral."*

Watered Down Christianity

Even in my brief stay on this earth, I have seen **churches lose their way** when it comes to sticking to **the message** of the Bible when it calls sin–**sin.**

What has become of the Holy Spirit led preacher calling for sinners to repent, accept Christ as their Savior and be born again? This sounds to me like a pretty fair assessment:

> *"In **many** churches", **A. W. Tozer** wrote, "Christianity has been **watered down** until the solution is **so weak** that if it were **poison** it would not hurt anyone and if it were **medicine** it would not cure anyone."*

Dangers of a Pluralistic Society

It did not take long for Israel to fall apart **spiritually** once they had entered the Promised Land. **God gives** freedom and choices to all, but **tolerance** cannot be the same as **approval,** which Israel did with the pagans in Canaan, and Christians oft times do with the things of the world. Soon Israel was **bowing to Baal** and *"**Christians** sometimes follow a similar road; first "**friendship**" with the world, then "**spoiled**" by the world, soon "**love**" for the world, then "**conforming**," and finally "**condemned**" with the world."*

Warren Wiersbe

CHAPTER THREE

Obedience and Heart Issues

Two Bible doctrines that challenge the faithful followers are the dynamics of God's desire for **obedience,** and His fondness for those who have **a heart for Him.** We all wish we had the honor of David and his place in the scriptures as *"a man after God's own heart."* But David was unique, but so are we, and God loves us just as much, warts and all. Oh by the way, old David had some obedience issues too, didn't he?

But I believe that obedience and things of the heart for God go hand in hand. What do I mean? Well, when we **disobey** God, it affects our **hearts**, and if our hearts are not right with God, obedience is just another **stumbling block**. This sometimes leads people to **think** they can circumvent obedience with **sacrifices, works, or deeds**. Sorry, but there are too many verses in God's Word that say otherwise, as I will point out later in the chapter. **Obedience** trumps **sacrifices.**

The **heart**, on the other hand, has limitless possibilities. Even many non-Christians recognize the heart's place in society and the **good deeds** many do for others is commendable. Sigmund Freud, not particularly known as a Bible scholar, said, "In the **small** matters, trust the **mind;** in the **large** ones the **heart."** Pretty good idea–right?

So, the thought that begs to be asked is: How much **more** should God's call for **obedience** affect people who love the Lord and see His clear call to **open their hearts** to His leading? I'll leave that question to the **only person** who knows the answer-**you.**

Great subjects upon which to **meditate.** Have a good walk...

God's Ever Watching Eye

We can never **fool God**, so why try? I forget where I found this gem but it says it all:

> *"He is looking on, taking notice of all, whether there be **integrity** of purpose, **intelligence** of mind, and **desire of heart** to please Him."* **Unknown**

Obey or Stumble

We are a **stubborn and wild** breed of Adam's children, are we not? Although God **has given us** in His Word all the information we will ever need to **be obedient**, this thought speaks for itself:

> *"Unwillingness to **obey** the Word makes **stumbling** a forgone conclusion."* **Unknown**

Heart and Life

There are a lot of **books to read** and many **places to seek** that propose to tell us the **best** path to follow in life, but **the bottom line** is this:

> *"Keep your **heart** with all **diligence,** for out of it spring the issues of life."* **Unknown**

A Contented Heart

In this age of **gathering riches** any way we can, from **the lottery to larceny,** here is a better idea:

> *"**Contentment** is really **greater** than riches, for if contentment does not produce riches, it achieves **the same object** by banishing **the desire** for them."* **Unknown**

The Enemy of the Heart

God has **much** to say about **pride.** Sadly, much of man's disobedience **and hard heartedness** begins with his **pride**— just ask **Lucifer...**

> *"Pride **keeps** a person **from turning to** God. Pride will not **acknowledge help** is needed from anyone, **human or divine.** Pride **intensifies all other sins,** because we **cannot repent** from any of them **without first giving up pride."***
>
> **Unknown**

Is Your King Home Today?

Here is a delightful little thought for those **who know** the King of Kings:

> ***"Joy is** the **flag** that flies above **the castle** of our hearts, announcing that **the King is in residence."***   **Unknown**

Obedience verses Sacrifices

I mentioned in **the introduction** of this chapter that there would be **more** concerning God's desire for **obedience** in place of **sacrifices**. Most of these references are from the Old Testament because that is where sacrifices **played a big part** in forgiveness **before** the shedding of blood by Christ. God never wanted sacrifices or gifts given **out of ritual or hypocrisy**, but **out of love and obedience**. Note the following references which **I hope** you will take the time **to look up:**

1 Samuel 15:22-23 *obedience far better than sacrifices.*

Psalms 40:6-8 *not burnt offerings but lifelong service.*

Psalms 51:16-19 *not public or private penance but a broken and repentant heart.*

Jeremiah 7:21-23 *not sacrifices but obedience and the promise He will be their God.*

Amos 5:21-24 *God hates hypocrisy, He wants justice to roll like a river.*

Micah 6:6-8 *offerings do not satisfy God, but what is right, mercy, and a humble walk.*

Matthew 9:13 *not sacrifices, but be merciful.*

The Obedient Servant

Did you know that **we are free** to be servants? That **great preacher** of the past, A. W. **Tozer** wrote this:

*"The ideal Christian is one who **knows** he is free to do as he wills–and wills to be **a servant**. This is the **very path that Christ took** and blessed is the man who **follows Him."***

Greedy Hearts

Moses **constantly** had to warn the children of Israel even before they **ever put a foot** into the Promised Land about remembering **where** their blessings all came from (**Deut. 8:10, 17-20**). The following comment from **Warren Wiersbe** should **warn all of us:**

> *"Idolatry begins in the heart when gratitude to the Giver is replaced by greediness for the gifts."*

Heartfelt Offerings

In **Isaiah 66,** God gets **quite graphic** with Isaiah about how He views **hypocrisy** and **false worship.** He makes it clear that it is **the heart** of the worshipper that determines **the value** of the offering. Someone said it this way:

> *"God does not live in buildings but dwells in the heart of those who submit to Him."*   **Unknown**

Giving from the Heart

When Nehemiah **had finished the wall** around Jerusalem, he then went about getting the people prepared to **worship** the Lord: putting away **sin**, and **giving** of the tithe so the Levites could run the temple.

Christians often **struggle** with the principals of **giving back to God.** Here is a little reminder to see what your temperature is:

> *"Giving is both the thermostat and the thermometer of the Christian life. It measures our spiritual temperature and also helps to keep it at the right level."*   **Unknown**

Obedience to Traditions

One of the **greatest examples** of obedience in all the Bible is found **in Jeremiah 35**. The context is this: The **sons of Jonadab,** the **son of Rechab**, had been commanded by their fathers to **never drink wine** or **live in houses**; they were nomads. They and their families had **all obeyed** for hundreds of years.

Judah, on the other hand, **God's chosen** people, had **disobeyed Him** at every turn. The **contrast** is fabulous reading and **the comparisons** are enlightening. Look:

1. The Rechabites (REE-kab-ites) **kept a vow to a fallible leader**; Israel would not obey an **infallible God**.

2. Told **not** to drink wine at any time, the sons of Jonadab **obeyed**; Israel was told **not** to sin, but sinned **constantly.**

3. Jonadab's sons **obeyed** for hundreds of years; Israel **disobeyed** for hundreds of years.

4. Jonadab's decendents would be **rewarded,** as seen in **verse 19**; Israel would be **punished** when Jerusalem fell and the children **went into captivity**.

The lesson is this: *If **temporal words** can be obeyed, why are **eternal laws** of God disobeyed? Today, **if Christians** put into **their** spiritual walk **what non-believers** put into **their** lives, the church would be alive and well. It all **starts with obedience.***

Choices and Consequences

Today's society is becoming **less Godly** and **more secular** by constantly passing more and more **anti-biblical laws**, prime example, same sex marriage. Christians may be facing **some tough choices** and **decisions in the future.** However, remember:

"A heart that ***loves*** *the Lord, and* ***trusts*** *the Lord, and therefore* ***obeys the Lord*** *has no difficulty making the* ***right choices*** *knowing He will* ***take care*** *of any consequences. Pure* ***faith*** *in God is* ***obeying*** *in spite of consequences."*

Unknown

God Comforts the Heart

The **heart** of man **seeks a comfort** that **only** the Creator can give.

French philosopher **Blaise Pascal** said, *"There is a* ***God-shaped vacuum*** *in the human heart,"* and **St. Augustine** observed, *"****You**** have made us O Lord,* ***for yourself,*** *and our* ***heart**** will find no rest until it* ***rests in you.***"

Obedience Sometimes Means Endurance

The Bible **tells us** over and over again that God's **major pursuit**, once we come to **know Him**, is **obedience.** This dynamic, visual observation comes from **Chuck Swindoll–**

"God is not some ***Divine Bellhop*** *waiting to* ***hear our order****, or a* ***Divine Genie*** *in a bottle, ready to* ***grant our every prayer uttered****. Instead,* ***His desire*** *is to create within His children* ***a capacity for endurance****. That capacity may be* ***cultivated*** *through hardship and disappointments, as well as* ***physical, or emotional, or heartfelt pain.***"

Important Bible Difference

Someone made this **thought provoking** prediction:

*"The important thing **at the judgment seat of Christ** won't be how much Bible we **studied or learned** but how much we **loved and obeyed.**"*

Truth or Lies?

Sad to say but **Warren Wiersbe** was right when he wrote: *"the **human heart** would rather **hear lies** that bring comfort **than truths** that bring conviction and cleansing."*

That thought **was born** out of **Ezekiel 3** where God sent Ezekiel the prophet to *"**all the house of Israel** who are **impudent and hard-hearted.**"* The issue was **how many prophets** God would have to send **before** Israel would **either repent or face judgment.**

Could we not ask the **same** question of America?

A Heart for People

I never knew my wife's father, **Bill Longwell** from Bath, New York. But I have heard **many** stories of his tireless **passion t**o help people **in need**. I'm told that **this note** was found in his wallet **when he died:**

*"Before life passes you by, **stop** and take time to **look around**, the beauty of the country side, your friends and family, and then **give thanks** that you can be part of it. Today and everyday **smile** and say **hello** to someone. It might make their day more enjoyable. **Pray** and give thanks for what **you** have. **May God bless you.**"*

Leigh C. Sweely

PERSONAL REFLECTION

The Crucifixion

Of all the subjects I taught, I must confess that the **most difficult** one was the crucifixion. Every year, prior to Easter, we were asked to teach lessons having to do with **Passion Week**. Now, if you really prepared yourself **spiritually** and **emotionally**, these lessons could have a sad, almost gloomy effect. **That is until** I came across this expository thought from **The Bible Believers Commentary by Wm. MacDonald** and the **comments of J. C. Ryle.** This put **everything** in a whole new light. Their summary of the crucifixion is: "It was **not** about the Romans, the thieves, Mary, the disciples, or any other **man-made** reason; it was totally and completely about: **Glory to the Father and Glory to the Son.**"

In order to **capture the essence** of this assessment, read carefully the following scripture, **John 17:1-5 (NKJV):**

Jesus spoke these words, lifted up His eyes to heaven, and said: "Father, the hour has come. Glorify Your Son, that Your Son may also glorify You. I have glorified You on the earth. I have finished the work You have given Me to do. And now, O Father, glorify Me together with Yourself, with the glory which I had with You before the world was."

Now, let's **break down** what **Jesus prayed**.

First, it was His **desire** to bring–

Glory to the Father

The crucifixion glorified the Father's **wisdom, faithfulness, holiness, and love.** Let's look closer:

Wisdom. It showed the Father **wise** in providing a plan whereby He could be **just** and still be **justifier** of the ungodly.

Faithful. It showed the Father **faithful** in keeping the **promise that the seed** of the woman would **bruise** the serpents head.

Holy. It showed the Father **holy** in requiring His **law's demands** to be satisfied by **our great Substitute.**

Love. It showed the Father's **love** in providing such a **mediator, redeemer, and friend** for sinful man: He offered **up His co-eternal Son.**

Second, Jesus also showed that **His desire** was to bring–

Glory to the Son

The crucifixion glorified Jesus' **compassion, patience, and His power.** Again, a closer look:

Compassion. It showed Jesus' most **compassionate** in dying for us, **suffering** in our stead, and allowing Himself **to be sin** and **a curse** for us plus buying our redemption with the **price of His own blood.**

Patient. It showed Jesus' **patience** by not dying a **common** death, but willingly submitting to the **pain and agony** of the cross when just a word could have **set Him free.**

Power. It showed Jesus' most **powerful**, bearing the weight of all **transgressions** of the world and by doing so, vanquishing Satan by **robbing him of his prey.**

Let us therefore remember daily when we think of the crucifixion: *"Jesus paid a debt **He didn't owe** because **we owe a debt we couldn't pay."***

PART TWO

*Personal Relationships
with God*

CHAPTER FOUR

Relationships: God/man–man/God–man/man

The dictionary describes a relationship as "A specified **state of affairs** existing among people related to or dealing with one another". Isn't it interesting that not one word is mentioned **about God** or **His relationship to man**. Christians believe that God created us, so that changes everything because our **personal** relationship to God is what really matters. It takes priority **over everything** else, for no one can afford to live or die under the frowning displeasure of God.

Thankfully, **God continues** to seek His lost sheep. This is quite obvious all the way back to the Book of Genesis. Remember **God's gentle voice**, in the cool of the day saying, "Adam, where are thou?" And God has continued to call, and to seek, and His voice has **never** died out.

But what about the lost sheep seeking **the Shepherd?** He loves it. Didn't Jesus say, *"Ask, and it will be given you; seek, and you shall find; knock, and it will be opened to you?"* Doesn't that sound like a **good Friend** who wants to have fellowship with you? Of course, and when we lift our eyes **towards heaven** seeking God, we can be sure there will be friendly eyes **looking back at us.**

And finally, what is to be our relationship with **our family, friends, and the family in God?** To be sure, **let's ask him.** If we look in His Word it says, *"**Honor** your father and mother,"* *"greater love has **no man** than this, to lay down **one's life for his friends,"*** and *"**if we** walk in the light as **He is in** the light, we **have fellowship** with one another."* **Any doubt** now about how He expects us to interact?

So, a relationship depends on at least **two parties.** Perhaps you will find something in the following thoughts that will give you a good reason to **strengthen, correct, or renew** a broken relationship, whether it be with the Lord or anyone else.

Are Relationships Really Necessary?

I want to **begin** this chapter with **a profound story** from **Joe E. Trull,** he wrote:

> *"We can **live** only in relationships. We **need** each other.* ***Really? Need proof?*** *Listen: A rather **crude and cruel** experiment was carried out by **Emperor Frederick,** who ruled the **Roman Empire** in the thirteenth century. He wanted to know what man's **original language** was: **Hebrew, Greek, or Latin?** He decided to **isolate** a few infants from* ***the sound*** *of the human voice.* ***He reasoned*** *that they would eventually speak the natural tongue of man. Wet nurses who were **sworn to absolute silence** were obtained, and though it was **difficult** for them, they **abided by the rule.** The infants **never heard a word–not a sound** from a human voice. What was the **final outcome?** Within **several months** they were **all dead.** "*

Conclusion: We not only **need each other** but man is a **spiritual** being, and in spite of what he **thinks,** he also **needs God.** There is **a "hole" in the soul** of **every human** ever born that **needs to be filled** with the One who **gave it.**

The Answer to Man's Problems with Each Other

There is a **constant battle** being fought between races, religions, ethnic heritage, and any number of other **differences** seen in each other. So, **as Christians**, what can we offer as **the answer?** Well, if you **believe the Bible,** and I do, **here** is the answer:

> *"The cross is God's answer to **racial discrimination, segregation, anti-Semitism, bigotry, and** every other **form of strife** between men."*   **Unknown**

Comforting Others

Feeling good about yourself and the world in general after a special morning **"quiet time"** with the Bible and the Lord is a great blessing. Now, what do you suppose **God expects** us to do with that new found manna? Well, here is a **"thought for today"**:

> *"When God comforts **our souls** we should **pass on** this comfort to others. We are **not comforted** to be **comfortable** but to comfort **others."*   **Unknown**

Man Rejects God

We are all **familiar** with the story of the Garden of Eden and how it has **affected** our relationship with God. How can we **put it down** on paper in its simplest form? I discovered this explanation somewhere:

*Man **is condemned by** God on **3 grounds:***

1. *He is sinful by nature.*

2. *Adam's sin is imputed to him.*

3. *He is a sinner by practice.*

*"But, his crowning guilt is his **rejection** of the provision **which God has made for his salvation, His Son, Jesus Christ."*** **Unknown**

Men Insulting God

If you study **Psalms 69:9 and Romans 15:3,** you will understand **Christ's disfavor** with men's evil remarks. **The heart** of this thought reflects that:

*"Jesus **lived** to please His Father, **not Himself.** He was completely taken up with **God's honor,** so that when sinful **men insulted God** He took it as a **personal insult** to Himself."* **Unknown**

Don't Blame the Lord

Here's **a short,** yet heart searching, poem from **Geoffrey O'Hara:**

Ye call me **"Master"** *and obey me not,*

Ye call me **"Lord"** *and serve me not,*

Ye call me **"The Way"** *and walk me not,*

Ye call me **"Truth"** *and believe me not.*

So if **I condemn** *thee,* **blame** *Me Not!*

All Creation Obeys God except Man

Luke, Chapter 8, is a telling story of **the difference** between **man** and **all other creations** of God.

"For when **Jesus exercised His lordship** *over the elements: the wind and waves* **(the storm)***, demons* **(the legions)***, disease* **(the blood issue)***, and even death* **(Jairus' daughter)***, all of* **these obeyed** *His commands.* **Only man refuses.** *Because man has been* **given a will** *to make* **choices,** *he does, and* **it is his undoing."***   **Unknown**

He Helps and Guides Us

We humans love to say, "I'd rather do it **myself**", even when it comes to the **things of the Lord.**

Remember this: *"God's providential working in our lives is both* **a delight** *and* **a mystery.** *God is constantly* **working with us** *(Mark 16:20),* **in us** *(Phil. 2:12-13), and* **for us** *(Rom. 8:28) to accomplish His gracious* **purposes."**

                Warren Wiersbe

When God Chastens

We are all familiar with **Hebrews 12:6**, *"For whom the Lord loves, He chastens."* That is a blessed verse, but sometimes people take God's chastening **personal** and withdraw from Him in **anger**. Maybe **this thought** will help if it happens **to you**:

> *"The **purpose** of God's chastening is **not punitive** but **creative**. He chastens "that we may **share** His holiness."* **Hebrews 12:10**.
>
> *His fire is a **refiner's fire**, and the **Refiner sits by it,** gently bringing **holiness** out of **carelessness**, and **stability** out of **weakness**. His love is **always in quest of purer things.**"*
>
> **Unknown**

Stubborn as an Ox

I have enough **Dutch blood** in me to sometimes be **stubborn and unmovable**; most times for the **wrong** reason. That is why **these thoughts** reminded **me of me**:

In **Daniel Chapter 4**, Nebuchadnezzar becomes like **an ox** and eats **grass.** Now some might ask–**is this possible?** Of course, and here's why:

> *"When Nebuchadnezzar let **pride** think **he** had made "**Babylon the Great**", God taught him a lesson **we all** must learn. God **alone** is sovereign and **we** are but **creatures;** He is the **creator,** we are only the **subjects;** and He **alone** is King of Kings. When we **refuse** to submit to the Creator, we are in danger of **descending** to the level **of animals.***

*King David warned: **do not** be like the horse or mule (**Psalm 32:9**), and yet he did **exactly that** when he became like the* *impulsive stallion* when he rushed into sin with Bathsheba and then a *stubborn mule* when he refused to **confess his sin.**

Remember **Saul (Paul)** on the Damascus Road was like a **stubborn ox** who God had to **prod** with **a goad** to make him **follow His leading.**

Christians have to always remember to **let God** do the leading. *He is our great* **Shepherd, but in His hand is a sturdy shepherd's hook.**"   **Warren Wiersbe**

Confess: We Do Not Know As Much as God

Wise Solomon wrote in **Proverbs 25:2,** *"It is the* **glory of God** *to conceal a matter…"* And if I may be **so bold as to add**, that is **His privilege** and **sovereign right.**

But **man thinks** he knows **more** than God and that is where the **relationship breaks down.** Man looks **at creation** and **refuses** to give God the credit and glory. No, man has it **all figured out because** he is **smarter than God.** This leads me **to confess** that I live on **a planet of fools,** the world **is overrun with them.**

Question: what has He **concealed** in **the heavens** and in **the bowels of the earth alone?** The answer is: **only He knows!**

Face to Face With God

The Bible is **quite clear** that we will **never see** the Father face to face; however, men **have seen Him** in the **person of Jesus Christ**, but that is a **whole other lesson.**

*But what has **happened when** man met God in **a deeper relationship? Moses trembled** on Mt. Sinai, **Isaiah declared** "woe is me," **Joshua and David** both fell on their faces, and **Daniel** became sick and weak.*

*In the New Testament, on the Mt. of Transfiguration, **Peter, James, and John** were filled with terror and fell on the ground. And **John**, who leaned **on Jesus' breast** at the Last Supper, fell at His feet **as though dead** when the **resurrected, King of Kings Jesus** appeared to him on the island of **Patmos.***

*When **God in His holiness** appears, all creation bows in **reverent fear.***

Serving God as a Caregiver

I love the **Book of Ecclesiastes.** In **Chapter 4,** Solomon looks at various **aspects of life** and one of these is for us to **look around** and **help others.**

Life can be **complex, difficult,** and **not always easy** to explain. If you don't believe me, **visit** some older souls and saints in **a nursing home.** Oft times they are **confused** and seek **any kind** of relationship **with anyone** who will give them **the time of day.** Many have **no one,** not one person *"who cares for my soul."*

But one thing **is sure:** *no matter where you **look**, you see **trials and problems**, and **people** who could **use some encouragement.*** Will **you** help?

Be Huggable

It got **a good laugh from my class** when I used this little example of **getting along** with others:

*In a "**Peanuts**" cartoon, **Lucy** says to **Snoopy**: "There are times when you really **bug me**, but I must admit there are also **times** when I feel like giving you **a big hug**".*

* **Snoopy** replies: "That's the **way I am**.....**huggable and buggable.**"*   **Robert Short,** *Parables of Peanuts*

God Surprised by Man?

If I can get you **to open the Word of God** to check out any of the **information or thoughts** in this book–**good!** So, in order to **understand this entry** please read **Psalm 33:10-11** to get the context of this thought:

*"God is **never surprised** or **caught off guard** by what people will **do, say, think, or plan.** I believe **this includes world leaders.** Therefore, He is **never at a loss** for what He must do. He will **always** have the **last word."*   **Unknown**

Family Relationships

Even **great men** of the Bible, called by God **to serve and lead** had problems within their own families.

Samuel's sons loved to line their own pockets and David's sons wanted to replace their father in authority. King Saul also had a dysfunctional family life and although Jonathan his son was a good soldier, God did not want Saul and David's lines to mix when it came to the ruling of Israel. Eventually, all of Saul's sons were eliminated from leadership.

As **fathers, mothers, grandparents,** we can only lead **by example**. If we know we have done **our best** for God, along with **prayer**, we have to leave **the results** in God's hands. However, a solid relationship is **a good start**.

A Bondservant of Christ

Here is a great question **to ponder**. Think about this: **how much** do we **owe** Christ for what he has **done** for us? Would you **volunteer** to be His servant? Can there be a relationship if one is a **servant?** The **answer** is - **absolutely**.

In **Luke 17:7-10,** Jesus tells His disciples **and us** what He expects **in service** for Him. **Roy Hession** spelled it out **beautifully** in his *The Five Marks of a Bondservant of Christ:*

1. *A bondservant must be **willing** to have one thing on top of another **put upon him** without **any consideration** being given him.*

2. *In doing this he must **understand** that he will **not be thanked**.*

3. *Having done all this, he must **not charge the Master** with selfishness.*

4. *He must **confess** that he is an **unprofitable servant**.*

5. *He must **admit** that doing and bearing all, it was done in **meekness and humility**, and he has **not done** one stitch more than it was **his duty to do**.*

*Why? Because **in the light of Calvary**, nothing we can ever do for the Savior **is sufficient** to **repay Him for what He has** done for us. Amen and Amen*

Leaders in Relationships

When it comes to **God's work**, leading the way can be tricky. Unless a person **is willing** to check their ego at the door it will not work. **Authority** in church requires **leadership, character,** and **integrity** plus a submissive attitude towards the Lord.

*"Leaders **without** these attributes can become **dictators** and abuse their power and **drive** God's people **like cattle** instead of **leading** them **like sheep**."* **Unknown**

Relationship with God Involves Work

In **Genesis** we read that God, **soon after** creating man, **put him to work**. Why? Because God **needed someone** to till the soil and tend the grounds **(Gen. 2:5 &15).**

*"That was **God's plan**–but man had **a better one**–let's give people **something for doing nothing,** and haven't we **seen the folly** of that? Even Christians need to **plant** by plowing, **sow** the seeds, **water** the words, and **pull** out the weeds. No amount of **prayer or Bible study** will replace true "**work**" for God."* **Unknown**

The Sovereignty of God

Spurgeon said, *"There is **no attribute of God** more **comforting** to His children than the doctrine of **divine sovereignty**. On the other hand, there is no doctrine more **hated** by the world."*

Why? Because **the human heart** is proud and **does not** want to **submit** to Almighty God.

Using Wisdom in Relationships

In **Deuteronomy Chapter 4,** Moses tells Israel that if they are to be **a great people** they must learn to **use God's wisdom and understanding.** Moses also added **love, gratitude,** and **separation from sin.**

> *"Wisdom is not just **head knowledge** but character as well, and **along with** relationships and responsibilities, this **teaches** our children and grandchildren **God's principals and morals.** This then becomes a **firm foundation** for any child to grow on."*   **Unknown**

Resisting God's Call

How can we **have a relationship** with God when, if He **calls,** we **hide, make excuses,** or **resist** in some other way?

Well, don't feel too bad because even **great men** in the Bible **resisted** God's call. Men such as **Moses, Gideon, Saul, Jeremiah,** and of course, **Jonah,** who all resisted.

In contrast, **Isaiah replied,** *"Here am I, **send me"** and* **Mary** said, *"I am the Lord's **maidservant.** Let it **be to me** according to **your word."***

> *"The man or woman **we think** least qualified for God's work **may turn out** to be a mighty servant for the Lord. What **will you do** if needed?"*   **Unknown**

Returned Relationships

Why is it **important** to **repent** and then **get back** to serving God even after some **serious** sin?

*A **perfect example is David**. He sinned mightily **with Bathsheba**, then **ignored** God's orders and sinned again when he **took a census** of Israel. But he repented before God and as a **result**: he purchased the property **on Mt. Moriah** to build an **altar** to God. He then had **another son** with Bathsheba named **Solomon**, who built the Temple. And his crowning glory was that he will always be known as "**a man after God's own heart.**"*

Paul said it perfectly in **Romans 5:20:** "Where **sin** abounds, **grace** abounded much more."

A Relationship with God Takes Time

There are **no shortcuts** to God. Modern Christians, sad to say**, think** they can have deeper spiritual connections with God in **short, easy lessons**. Not so. The hard **truth** is that God wants our **heart, soul, and mind** devoted to Him, and **that requires time.**

*"Many **saints of old** spent hours in **meditation and prayer**. They never **skipped through** the marketplace like so many **children**. So Christian, **set apart** some part of your day, every day, and **spend it with God."***   **Unknown**

The Bread of Life Discourse

The latter part of **John, Chapter 6,** is when the Lord changes from **simple fellowship** to **true discipleship**. Jesus began His ministry with **fairly simple** teachings. As He progressed, it became apparent the Jews were **rejecting** His words. The more they closed their hearts and minds to the **truth**, the more **difficult** His teachings became. When the discourse of the eating of **flesh** and drinking of **blood** was expounded, it was too much for them and they said, *"**Who** can **understand** it?"* and walked away.

*"**Rejection** of the truth results in **spiritual blindness**. Because they **would not** see, soon they came to the place where they **could not see**."* **Unknown**

Honest Seekers or Rejecters

This is an important **follow-up** to the previous thought.

Verse **66** of **John 6** says, *"From that time **many** of His disciples went back and **walked with Him no more.**"* Keep in mind that these were **not** just hangers-on or friends, the verse says they were **"disciples,"** men who had become **close followers.** Then Jesus asked **the** 12 disciples, *"Do **you also** want to go away?"*

Really Christian, there is **no middle ground** with Jesus. Even the 12 could have **rejected Him.** His teachings were **not intended** to repel; Christ was simply telling **the truth** about how men **must spiritually** consume His message, body, and blood.

*"His true message **divided His listeners** into two different camps; **honest seekers** who wanted to understand more, and those who **rejected Him** because they **didn't like what they heard."***   **Warren Wiersbe**

CHAPTER FIVE

The Leading and Power of the Holy Spirit

The Bible has much to say about the third Person of the Trinity, the Holy Spirit. If you are reading this and you can clearly testify of **being born again**, having Christ as your personal Savior, **you have Him** in you, guiding and leading your path every day.

Due to weak preaching in many of today's churches, the people never hear about the **new birth and the filling** of the Holy Spirit. Hence, many lost people today are **unaware** of the Holy Spirit's role in the salvation of sinners. The scriptures are very clear: we are **drawn** by, **convicted** by, **born** of, and **kept** by the Holy Spirit.

Scripture tells us He helped **launch the early church**, propped up **Paul** when the whole world was against him, **and led the writers of the New Testament** to proclaim *"all that Jesus said and did."* In return, when the scribes and Pharisees attributed the healing of a demon possessed man to the power of Satan, Jesus advised them they had committed the *"unpardonable sin"* of **blasphemy** against the Holy Spirit of God.

Finally, as a word of testimony, I know from **personal experience** those occasions when I have felt His leading and power while doing the Lord's work. What a joy to **experience an "aha" moment,** knowing that what just happened was **a God thing.** There are examples of these "reflective moments" scattered throughout this book: I think you will find them interesting.

Now here is the neat part: some of **the following thoughts and entries** were also "aha" moments. I hope the same thing **happens to you.**

What Fills Your Cup?

When we describe the work of the Holy Spirit we often use the word **"filling."** How it applies to our lives is captured here:

*"To be filled with **a new** ingredient a cup must first be emptied of **the old**. To be filled **with Him,** we must first be emptied **of us.**"* **Unknown**

Christ First

A good follow-up concerning the previous thought:

*"The ministry of Christ through the Holy Spirit **does away with I, Me, and my.**"* **Unknown**

Christians are privileged

Peter went all the way back to **the Book of Leviticus 11:44:** to remind the people that God said, *"Be Holy, for I am Holy."* How does that apply to today?

*"Today we have the Holy Spirit as a Help Mate; the Old Testament saints did not. Therefore, since we are more **privileged**, we are more **responsible.**"* **Unknown**

We Have the Power

When you have the Holy Spirit you possess the **unseen something** needed to succeed. The following quote sums it up well:

*"**The task** ahead of you is never as great as **the Power** behind you."* **Unknown**

The Holy Spirit and the Law

Many modern Christians get nervous whenever **the Law** is brought into New Testament conversations. But the Law is what **convicts people of their sin** and then the Holy Spirit uses conviction to lead sinners to the Savior. **Billy Graham** explains that so well:

> *"The Holy Spirit **convicts us**...He shows us the 10 Commandments; the Law is **the schoolmaster** that leads us **to Christ**. We look in the mirror of the 10 Commandments, **and we see ourselves in that mirror.**"*

A Heavenly Gift

Jesus is speaking here when He told us, *"If you then, being evil, know how to give good gifts **to your children**, how much more will your heavenly Father **give the Holy Spirit** to those who **ask Him!**"* (Luke 11:13) There are at least two wonderful truths here:

1. *A gift from our heavenly Father **that we need** and one He most desires to **give** is the Holy Spirit. We should pray that we are **teachable**, can be **guided**, and that His power will be poured out on us in **our service** for Christ.*

2. *Jesus said it will be given **"to those who ask Him."** Man's free will comes into play here. Our heavenly Father **will give**, but we **must ask**.*

Spreading the Word

The Book of Acts is full of the stories and examples of the early church and their dependence on the Holy Spirit. *"You will be my witnesses in Jerusalem and in Judea and Samaria, and to the end of the earth,"* (Acts 1:8), which caused **theologian J. I. Packer** to pen this thought:

"The Holy Spirit is God the evangelist."

The Spirit's Role in Salvation

That great voice for God, **Charles Spurgeon** (1834-1892) spoke these words:

*"You might as well expect to **raise the dead** by whispering in their ears, as hope to save souls by preaching to them, if it **were not for the agency of the Spirit.**"*

The Spirit Longs to Use Us

We err brethren if we **do not use** the power given us by the Spirit **for God's kingdom**. Listen to what **T. J. Bach, a director of The Christian and Missionary Alliance Church** wrote:

*"The Holy Spirit longs to reveal to you **the deeper things** of God. He longs to **love** through you. He longs to **work** through you. Through the blessed Holy Spirit you may have: **strength** for every duty, **wisdom** for every problem, **comfort** for every sorrow, and **joy** in His ever flowing service."*

Life without the Spirit

What insight God gave to that Yankee farm boy, **Dwight L. Moody** (1837-1899). Listen:

> *"You might as well try to **hear without ears,** or **breathe without lungs,** as try to live a Christian life **without** the Spirit of God in your heart."*

Methods or Power?

God's man for inland China, **J. Hudson Taylor** said:

> *"We have given too much attention to **methods** and to **machinery** and to **resources,** and too little to the **Source of Power, the filling with the Holy Ghost."***

A Hand in a Glove

Here is **a delightful yet very profound example** of us using the power of the Holy Spirit:

> *"I have a glove here in my hand. The glove cannot do anything **by itself,** but when my hand is **in** it, it can **do many things.** True, it is not the glove, but my hand **in the glove** that acts.*
>
> **We** are gloves. It is the Holy Spirit **in us** who is **the hand, who does the job.** We have to **make room** for the hand so that every finger **is filled."***   **Corrie ten Boom**–*Dutch Christian*

Are You Tuned In or Tuned Out?

I found this story and commentary tucked away in my library I have saved over the years. It was from **Jane Driscoll**, a student in my adult Bible Study at First Baptist of Sarasota, Florida. It goes as follows:

*When I was growing up, I stayed with my grandparents for a week or two every summer. They lived on a street that dead-ended into **some railroad tracks**. I would often awaken several times the first night as the box cars rumbled by or when the engineer blew the whistle. By the end of my visit however I had **grown accustomed** to the noise and could sleep straight through the night without interruption. **I had tuned out the sounds.***

*Sometimes we're tempted to tune out **"divine interruptions"** by the Holy Spirit. He may nudge us with the realization that we need to **ask forgiveness** for something we had said or did. Or He may persistently **remind us** that we should pray for someone who is going through a crisis, or convict us that we had not shared Jesus with a person we really care about. When the **Holy Spirit indwells, teaches, convicts, comforts, and guides** us into truth, we **always need to be "tuned in."***

Listening

Jane had also sent this short little poem in the same context:

*Holy Spirit, **help us hear***
*Your **inner promptings**, soft and clear;*
*And help us know **your still, small voice***
*So we may make God's will **our choice**.*   **D. DeHaan**

PERSONAL REFLECTION

Those "Aha" Moments

To have a personal relationship with the Lord is one thing. To experience that **undeniable** euphoria one feels when you **"know"** God has guided you through an **action, prayer, or need** is another. Those who have experienced the latter understand what I mean about an **"aha" moment.** Allow me to give you an example:

On Thursdays, I visit with residents of an assisted living and elderly nursing home. I am part of a volunteer ministry under **the Chaplin's office** and our job is to just sit and talk, reminisce, and read scripture to folks who **need some cheer** in their lives.

Let me tell you about **Dorothy.** She is in her late 80s, can **barely hear**, is **bed ridden**, and **blind.** And yet this dear heart is **as cheerful** as anyone I know. She makes a fuss over each and every visit and **hugs** me and **kisses** me on the cheek whenever I leave.

Several weeks ago, she was in a **rather somber mood** and said to me, "I pray and **ask God** all the time to give me my sight back. Do you think God **will answer me** so that I will someday see again?"

Tough question, but I replied, "Dorothy, **can He** heal you? **Yes**, but **will He chose** to do it now, I don't know. But I **do know** that we need to have **faith** that whatever **God chooses** for us is best. Besides, when you **get to heaven** think how amazing it will be because **the first thing** you will **see** will be the **face of Jesus.**"

That seemed to **satisfy her.** Since our visit was about over I asked her **what scripture** she would like for me to read to her. She said, "**John**, something from the **gospel of John** would be nice." So I opened the latter half of my Bible and it opened directly to **John**. I looked down and read to her, **John 9:1**, *"Now as Jesus passed by, He saw a man who was blind from birth."* Needless to say, I was **speechless,** yet felt tremendously **blessed** at the same time.

Someone has said that a **"coincidence"** when doing the Lord's work is really the Holy Spirit working **behind the scenes.** The best part is that more coincidences keep happening the more you serve God, better known as **"aha"** moments.

So often over the years I have visited **to uplift the elderly** and it turns out that **I am** the one **who winds up** with the blessing. It can be the same for you if you pray for meaningful work to do for the Lord.

PART THREE
Christian Triumphs

CHAPTER SIX

Keys to Victory–Faith and Prayer

F-A-I-T-H. A five letter word upon which **much** of Christianity **stands.** Simply put, it is a **belief in** or confident attitude **towards God** involving a commitment to His will for one's life. The shining example that Bible lovers always use is **Hebrews, Chapter 11.**

Here the heroes of faith are proudly displayed beginning with **Abraham** who *"believed in God,"* and his seed of **Isaac, Jacob, and Joseph.** They were followed in succession by men and women who would be examples for centuries to come.

New Testament faith covers **various levels** of personal commitment. That slight note of **difference** is important because today **liberals and Bible doubters** teach that mere **intellectual agreement** to **a truth** is all one needs. That foolish notion is shattered by **James 2:19,** because when it comes to God and belief, *"even the demons believe–and tremble."* No, **true Bible faith** is the confidence that His Word is **true,** Christ is our **Rock,** and **faith in self** is **folly.**

Prayer, the other bookend of this chapter, must be **a strong and daily part** of our lives. Prayer is essential if we are to walk the walk and talk the talk. Christians recognize their **dependence**

upon God and need to pray and communicate with Him **daily.** Prayer expresses so many things to God; **gratitude for His blessings, love, worship, confession, needs,** and the list goes on and on. If you are a true **prayer warrior,** you know what I am trying to say. **Without prayer,** we are empty.

Now, let's examine what others have said and written about **faith and prayer.** I have **faith** that there will be **something** within this chapter that you can claim for yourself and my **prayer** is that God will use it to **His glory.** Amen and amen.

Faith Verses Fact

I have taught many classes **about faith.** Here is one of the best, down to earth examples I have found that works with a full classroom of students;

> *"That you are sitting here with me in this room* **is a fact.** *That I am standing in front of you to teach* **is a fact.** *But it is only* **faith** *that makes me believe* **anyone is listening."**
>
> **Anonymous**

What's On Your Prayer List?

People sometimes **wonder** whether or not to pray about something that may **seem incidental or unimportant.** Here's a suggestion that I picked up somewhere-

> **"Everything** *should be taken to the Lord in prayer. Everything means everything. Prayer is both an* **act** *and an* **atmosphere.** *We should be* **anxious** *in nothing,* **prayerful** *in everything,* **thankful** *for anything."*

Faith That Carries On

A **true test** of a person's faith comes when the sky falls in on him or her. In the following example, it is not about health problems but **daily bread** issues. So according to the Bible, what is the child of God to do? Try this–

> *"It is a* **blessed secret** *when the believer learns to carry his* **head high** *with an* **empty stomach,** *look* **up** *with an* **empty pocket,** *have a happy heart with* **no salary,** *and* **joy** *in God when other men have* **no hope."*   **Unknown**

Think of Prayer as a Privilege

Let's get real for a moment. **Think** of yourself as just a **grain of sand** on a wide beach. You are in reality a speck of nothing, but God knows **each and every one** of us personally and individually. So when you pray, you have **His full attention.** With that in mind, let this thought settle into your soul—

*"Prayer is the **unspeakable privilege** of having an audience with the **Sovereign of the Universe,** the Father of our Lord Jesus Christ. The One who is **infinitely high** has become intimately nigh."*   **Unknown**

Which Way Are You Faced?

Someone has said that you *"pray as **your face** is set–towards **God** or towards **the world.**"*

The Bank of Faith

The world crisis in the **banking industry** began about 2008 and is still being felt today. It caused many people to **lose faith** in a **world system**. But **the Christian** has a **different** bank and a better **promissory note.**

Let's look at **what Paul said** in **Philippians 4:19,** *"My God shall supply all your need according to His riches in glory by Christ Jesus."* Now, let's **break this down** and treat it as **a note** drawn upon **The Bank of Faith**:

"**My God**–*the **name** of the Banker.*

Shall supply–*the **promise** to pay.*

All your need–*the **value** of the note.*

According to His riches–*the **capital** of the bank.*

In glory–*the **address** of the bank.*

By Christ Jesus"–*the **signature** at the foot, **without which the note is worthless.***   **Unknown**

Food for Faith

Probably a week doesn't go by without **some type** of testing concerning our faith. But this is where our **inner strength** comes in, listen–

*"Faith **is confidence** in the trustworthiness of God. It is **the conviction** that what God says is true and what He promises **will come to pass**. God tests our faith to see if it **is genuine**. Always remember that **difficulties** are **food for faith** to feed on."*   **Unknown**

A Thought from My "Cousin"

The following quote comes from my "Christian cousin" **Bob Williams.** Bob and I had a lot in common: both from **Pennsylvania,** shared the same **last name,** liked to **cook,** loved **Penn State** football (Go Nits!). When my spiritual brother died several years ago after a courageous bout with cancer, I looked for and found a quote he had handed me before Adult Bible Study class one Sunday. Here it is–

*"People may **mock our message** but they are **helpless** against our **prayers.**"*

Amen and thanks Cuz…

Patient Faith of Ruth

There is a tremendous exchange in the Bible story of Ruth between **Naomi and Ruth** (Ruth 3:16-18).

Sometimes we, like Ruth, get **in the way** of God's working by our impatience. Naomi's advice to Ruth was to *"Sit **still,** my daughter, until you **see** how the matter will turn out."*

The clear lesson is this: *"For **the believer,** oft times **the most difficult** part of faith, when **nothing more** can be done, is to **wait patiently** for God to work. We must **not** allow **doubts to rise** and **anxiety to creep in.**"*   **Warren Wiersbe**

Esther's Faith Rewarded

From Ruth to Esther is an interesting change in Bible stories. The Book of Esther, with all its **intrigue** and **plots** has Esther right **in the middle** when Haman, the villain, tries to have her Uncle Mordecai condemned. Esther has a **plan,** but if it doesn't work, she **will surely die.** *"If I perish, I perish"* this brave woman said.

Think about **what her faith** was up against as noted by **Warren Wiersbe:**

*"The **law** was against her because she planned to **interrupt the king.***

*The **government** was against her because all Jews were **to die.***

*Her **sex** was against her because women were **not to speak** without being addressed first.*

*The **officers** were against her because Haman had them all **in his pocket.***

*And even **her plan to fast and pray** could backfire if she looked **anything but lovely** to the king.*

*But **we know** that, "if God be for us, who can be against us?" The **answer of faith** is–Nobody!*

Moses and Faith

There are many faith references in **Hebrews 11** because it is called the **"hall of fame"** among the Bible faithful. This thought is perfect when we consider the **faith of Moses–**

*"He was able to **see** the invisible, **choose** the imperishable, and **do** the impossible."* **V. Havner**

Faith and Circumstances

Here's some good sound Christian **common sense** that someone put on paper–

> *"Becoming a Christian **does not** protect us from the "**circumstances of life.**" But our faith should enable us **to look** at our circumstances through **the reality of God** and this gives us **hope**. Our circumstances **change,** and so do our feelings about them, but God is always **good, loving, and merciful.** To **build our lives** on the changeless and eternal God is to have **peace** and **contentment** and **hope."***

The Greatest Virtue?

What **Hebrews 11** is to **faith, 1 Corinthians 13** is to **love.** Listen to what verse 13 says, *"So now faith, hope, and love abide, these three; but the greatest of these is love."* Follow this though about all three:

> *"To love means loving **the unlovable.** To forgive means pardoning **the unpardonable.** Faith means believing **the unbelievable.** Hope means hoping when **everything seems hopeless."***

Gilbert Keith Chesterton (1874-1936)

Faith and Fear

Before going into the **Promised Land** the first time, Moses had the priests eliminate all those who were **too frightened** to fight. This thought seems right on target:

*"Fear and faith **cannot co-exist** successfully in the same heart because fear will **contaminate all the others**."*   **Unknown**

A great New Testament follow-up is found in **Matthew 8:26, Jesus** asked the same question of **His disciples,** *"Why are you **fearful** and where is your **faith?**"*

Shared Faith from Opposite Women

Here's another interesting example from **Hebrews 11:**

There are **only two women** named in the "Faith Hall of Fame," **Sarah and Rahab.** How could they possibly be any more **different?** Sarah, the **wife of the great patriarch Abraham**, and Rahab the **harlot of Jericho.** Someone offered this comment–

*"Humanly speaking, they are eons apart, but in **God's eyes** they shared a **divine point–faith.**"*

Faith and Feelings

As people of faith, **we** cannot **ignore** certain feelings when it comes to the **things of God.** While it is true we cannot let our emotions **get away** from us, on the other hand we cannot **suppress them** and become a **religious robot.** Here's a thought someone had–

*"Your life is only **as big as** your faith, and your faith is only **as big as your God.** So let God control the changing weather and the great **storms of life,** so that He may use it to show His people that their **faith is real.**"*   **Unknown**

Prayer = Communication with God

With that simple title, I want to list some of the **aspects of prayer** that the Bible speaks about. The scriptures are full of **great prayers** from **great people** but **the perfect prayers** were the **prayers of Jesus.** Perhaps there is something here you were unaware of, take a look:

Reasons for Prayer

- God's command to do so (Romans 12:12, 1 Tim. 2:8)
- The example of Christ, the early church, and Paul (Heb. 5:7, Acts 1:14, Rom. 10:1)
- Defeats the devil (Luke 22:32)
- Saves the sinner (Luke 18:13)
- Restores the backslider (James 5:16)
- Strengthens the believer (Jude 20)
- Heals the sick (James 5:13-15)
- Glorifies God's name (Rev. 5:8)
- Gives wisdom and peace (James 1:5, Phil. 4:5-7)

Hindrances to Prayer

- Sin not confessed (Psalms 66:18)
- Insincerity (Matt. 6:5)
- Carnal motives (James 4:3)
- Unbelief (James 1:5-6)
- Satanic activities (Daniel 10: 10-13)
- Domestic problems (1 Peter 3:7)
- Pride (Luke 18:10-14)
- Robbing God (Malaki 3:8-10)
- Refusal to submit to Biblical teaching (Proverbs 1:24-28)
- Refusal to forgive or to be forgiven (Matt. 5:23-24, 6:12,14)
- Refusing to help the needy (1 John 3:16-17)

Spiritual Aspects
- Faith–trust in His Word (Mark 11:22-24)
- Worship–God is Holy (Isaiah 6:3)
- Confession–sinfulness (Isaiah 6:5, Psalms 51:4)
- Adoration–for love and patience (Matt. 22:37)
- Thanksgiving–for forgiveness, grace, and mercy (Romans 1:21, Col. 3:17)
- Requests–for others and self (Isaiah 58:9-10)
- Affects–inner needs, strength, and guidance (Psalms 118:5-6, 138:3)

Personal Requirements
- Must have personal relationship with God (John 3:16)
- Have purity of heart (Psalms 66:18-19)
- Have a humble heart (Luke 18:13-14)
- Belief prayer will be heard (Hebrews 11:6)
- Be persistent (Luke 18:7)
- Offered in Christ's name (John 14:13-14)
- Within God's will (1 John 5:14)

Posture
- Standing (Nehemiah 9:5)
- Kneeling (Ezra 9:5)
- Sitting (1 Chron. 17:16-27)
- Bowing (Ezra 34:8)
- Hands up lifted (1 Tim. 2:8)

Things to Pray for
- Ourselves (Matt. 14:30, Luke 23:42)
- One another (James 5:16, Romans 1:9)
- Pastors (Ephesians 6:19-20)
- Sick believers (James 5:14-15)
- Rulers and nation (1 Tim. 2:1-3)
- Our enemies (Matt. 5:44)
- Israel–Jerusalem (Psalms 122:6, Isaiah 62:6-7)

As noted earlier, there are some great prayers recorded in the Bible **but the greatest**, in my humble opinion, is **Christ's prayer in John 17** on the night of His betrayal. We have the unbelievable **privilege** to listen as Jesus speaks directly to His Father.

*The disciples were one of the main focuses of His prayer and look what happened to them; they **turned the world upside down** for Him and **all but John** died a martyr's death for their faith in Him.*

That, my Christian friend, was their **conviction** of who He was and the **power of His prayer.**

Waiting in Faith

Have you ever waited on something spiritual that you thought was **good and right** but did not want to **rush** to a conclusion? So, **how patient** were you?

Christians can be a **restless lot**, and I believe that we (including myself) are unwilling at times to just **"calm down and wait."** This then puts us in **conflict** with the Bible because true biblical faith is oft times waiting for **God's time** and not **ours.** Next time, before you act on your decision, ask yourself these four questions:

1. *Am I **willing** to wait?*
2. *Am I **concerned only** for the glory of God?*
3. *Am I **obeying** God's Word?*
4. *Will I **have** God's joy and peace within?*

Think about how **longsuffering** God is with **us.** Can we return a **portion** to Him through faith, by waiting? Think about it....

The School of Faith

Genesis 22:1 says, *"God tested Abraham."* We too must have occasional **tests** or we will never see where **we stand spiritually.** In one sense, it is **a compliment** when God sends us a test; it shows us that God wants to **promote us** in "The School of Faith." God never sends a test until He knows we are **ready for it.**

> *"So, **lesson one,** expect tests and trials because the Christian walk is **not easy.** It wasn't for Jesus and **we are told** to walk in **His footsteps."*** **Warren Wiersbe**

Daniel's Prayer Example

Daniel was one of the outstanding **models** of a prayer warrior. Several times, except for the **intervening of the Lord,** he would have been killed because of his commitment to his prayer life. Here is another thought offered by another prayer captain–

> *"We should **pray for a faith** that will not **shrink** when washed in **the waters of afflictions."***

Kneeling in Prayer

From **Daniel** we go to another Bible hero, **Nehemiah.** Using him as an example, consider the fact that there are **three kinds** of people in the world:

1. Those who **don't know** what is happening.

2. Those who simply **watch** what is happening.

3. And those who **make** things happen.

"Nehemiah made things happen by **starting on his knees** before his God, sometimes **weeping.** But when he **rose to his feet,** he volunteered to **lead men** in an epic struggle. The person who **knows how to kneel in prayer** has no problem **standing** in the strength of the Lord."   **Warren Wiersbe**

Confessional Prayers

We're on a roll here with **godly examples,** so let's include one more: **Ezra.**

He was one of the **strong leaders** that God needed to lead His people **back** to Israel after the 70 years of **captivity.** Ezra's prayer was for forgiveness of **Israel's sins,** especially those that they had carried back **from Babylon to Jerusalem.** His prayer is a classic example of **simple, humble, remorseful confession.** Would to God we had an Ezra praying **for America.**

Spurgeon has said– *"It's the **strength** of our prayers, not the **length** of our prayers that is important."*

Faith Means Being Faithful

What has become of **the faithful** who still think that Sunday should be **the Lord's Day?**

Even within my lifetime, the **falling away** has been troubling. Does that mean people have just **lost their faith** (as in caring, not salvation) or is the failure **within the walls** of the church?

Apparently this must be **an old problem** because I found this thought from **William Gurnall** (1617-1679) who said, *"How can there be **great faith** where there is **little faithfulness.**"*

Prayer and God's Will

It has been well said that prayer is not getting **man's will done** in heaven, but getting **God's will** done on earth. There are **two** thoughts here:

1. *In order to* **have His will done** *on earth He must* **have people** *available for Him to use. Also, to* **answer** *prayer, He must* **start** *by working in the one doing the praying. Therefore, He works* **in us** *and* **through us** *so that we* **can see** *our prayers answered.*

2. *The other aspect is* **obedience and endurance** *as well as the realization that sometimes He will* **refine us** *through the* **fires of pain, suffering, or illness.**   **Unknown**

Some of God's **greatest saints** have been those who were **persecuted, handicapped or disabled.** Think **Joni Eareckson Tada, Dietrich Bonhoeffer, Fanny Crosby, Amy Carmichael,** and all the **martyrs** for Christ over thousands of years. Which brings us to this thought:

"Prayer should **not** *be a matter* **of personal convenience** *but of* **self-discipline and sacrifice."**   **Unknown**

Silent Prayer

If you recall the story of **Hannah** in 1 Samuel, she was so fervent in her **silent yet powerful** prayer to God that the priest **Eli thought** she was drunk (1 Sam. 1:13). Her prayer without words gives **this thought for today–**

"In prayer it is **better** *to have* **a heart** *without words than* **words** *without a heart."*   **John Bunyan**

Touching in Faith

One of my personal **favorite stories of faith** is the woman with **the blood issue** as told in Mark 5:24-34.

You know the scene: all the people **pressing about** Jesus as He walked toward the home of **Jairus,** the leader of the synagogue, whose daughter was dying. A **frail woman,** suffering **for years** with a female disorder, desperately **touches His robe** hoping for His healing power. **Her faith** cannot be denied even by Christ Himself, and she is **healed** on the spot. He, knowing deity had **gone out of Him,** confronts her and tenderly calls her "**daughter**" and assures her that it **was her faith** that made her well.

All that was written so that **this thought** can be appreciated, *"The flesh throngs, but faith touches."*   **Unknown**

By Faith or by Sight

You and I know lots of people who **say** they would believe if they could **see a miracle,** but they are mistaken.

Faith **is not based on senses,** but on the living Word of God. The attitude that **demands a sign** is not pleasing to God. That is **not faith** but sight.

Unbelief says, *"Let me see* and *then I will believe."* **God** says, *"Believe* and *then you will see."*   **Unknown**

Preparation for Prayer

Our **preparation for prayer and worship** is as important as the prayer itself, for without **a heart** that is **right** with God, our prayers are just so many **pious words**. An Unknown author said:

*"We need to **focus** on God's character and not be **preoccupied** with **ourselves** and our **burdens**. Then, if any do **persist** or we cannot seem to **break out** of the Satan's net, give it all to the Lord."*

CHAPTER SEVEN

Individual and Personal Reminders

The theme behind this chapter title is **my** personal **walk and pilgrimage** with the Lord. I emphasis **my walk** because these thoughts were saved because they meant something special to me. I'm sure if you had **your own collection,** your list would be completely different than mine, and **that's good**. God made no two people alike and our journey with Him must be an **oneness journey.**

When we consider **the Trinity,** it is easy to see how this works.

God the Father is the glue that holds everything together, from the vast outreach of the **universe** to the smallest **DNA,** and yet we have the **assurance** that He will hear each and every prayer.

God the Son, Jesus Christ, we know from scripture that when He walked this earth He constantly interacted with multitudes, **but** He also had time for **the woman at the well, Nicodemus, and the thief on the cross.**

God in the person of the Holy Spirit always deals with the individual. In fact, when He deals with me, He only deals **with me**, and when He deals or talks to **you**, it is **to you and you alone** and that is a special blessing to know.

So, **share** these thoughts that jumped out at me as I hope some will jump out to you. It would be neat to have **a common bond in the Lord.**

Early Risers and Spiritual Diaries

I believe **two keys** concerning our daily walk with the Lord are:

1. *The need to serve God **early in the day**, and*

2. *Keep a **spiritual diary** so that you don't forget special moments.*

Being an "early riser" puts you **in the same company** as Abraham, Jacob, Moses, Joshua, Samuel, Job, David, and **our Lord Jesus (Mark 1:35)**. Check it out.

At my age, I have to **write things down**. I write in my Bible notes I think will help me remember **a thought provoking truth** from scripture. Also, **special lessons** of life, **a spiritual truth,** or a **faith issue** that jump off the pages at me are fun to "nail down" and keep for future reference.

Who Has Your Trust?

As a red blooded American, I must admit I have been very upset recently with **the leadership** and the **direction** of this great land. However, the writer **of Psalms 146:3** reminds me, **"Do not** put your trust in princes…" and may I include **presidents, Congress, the courts, and even some preachers.** Here is a thought someone wrote along those lines:

*"The **best** of men **are men** at best. Unreliable, dysfunctional, immoral, and fleeting **in all ways.**"*

Orderly Lives

As a teacher, this caught my eye;

*"In our lives there should be the **order** of: teaching and **doing,** doctrine and **duty**, preaching and **practice**."*   **Unknown**

Our Great Gain

If only those who are working so hard for **"the finer things of life"** would understand what this Unknown writer meant when they wrote the following:

*"All **financial** gain, all **material** gain, all **physical** gain, all **intellectual** gain, all **moral** gain, all **religious** gain–all these are **no** gains at all, compared with **The Great Gain, Christ Jesus.**"*

Never Feel Satisfied

We should **never** feel that we have **"arrived"** in our Christian walk. Listen:

*"**Even Paul**, realizing that he had **not** attained perfection in Christ, said, "but I **press on**...Phil. 3:12. The lesson here is that **satisfaction** is the **grave of progress.**"*   **Unknown**

Independent Joy

Here's a thought some anonymous saint wrote about when life has you down:

*"Christian joy is a **mood independent** of our **immediate circumstances.** No matter how dark the circumstances of life may be, it is **always possible** for the Christian to **"rejoice in the Lord."***

A Rich Fool

In **Luke 12:16-21,** Jesus recounts the parable of the **rich man** who would tear down his barns to build bigger ones to store his excess crops. God said to him, *"Fool! This night **your soul** will be required of you."*

Someone commented:

*"The **bosoms of the poor,** the **houses of the widows,** the **mouths of the children** are **the barns** that last forever."*

Who is First in Your Life?

What is the **number one** thing in your life? Spouse, children, home, car, boat, money?

*"The Bible, and in fact **Jesus Himself,** made it very clear that He **cannot be second** anywhere. Creation and redemption hand the **honors of supremacy** to Him because of **who He is,** and **what He has done."*** Unknown

No Loners in Life

Many people claim they just want to **be alone,** not be bothered by anyone. That is certainly their privilege, but as **a child of God** we were made in His image, and hence:

*"No one **lives** to himself, and no one **dies** to himself. We cannot measure the range of our influence. We have **limitless potential** for **good or for evil."*** Unknown

Christian Good Works

The story of the **Wesley family** should be read by everyone who has an interest in the things and ways of God. **John Wesley**, one of the founders of the **Methodist church** penned this:

*"Do all the **good** you can, by all the **means** you can, in all the **ways** you can, in all the **places** you can, at all the **times** you can, to all the **people** you can, **as long as ever** you can."*

Humble Service

I love sports, but I have to admit that today's athletes need a dose of "humbleness" medicine. Whenever they do something **worthy of cheers,** it is all about "look what I did!"

Christians, remember this:

*"In God's Word we read repeatedly that whoever **exalts himself** will be **humbled,** and he who **humbles himself** shall be **exalted."***   **Unknown**

What is Repentance?

As sons and daughters of Adam and Eve, we **cannot escape** our sinful nature. God will always return us to His fellowship when we **truly repent and confess.** Somewhere I came across this definition of repentance:

*"A change of **mind,** which produces a change of **attitude,** an awareness of **conscience,** and this results in a change of **action."***   **Unknown**

Times of Testing

Israel went through a lot of **testing** during the Exodus. Often God put them to the test to develop their **maturity and spiritual growth**. We are no different, but keep in mind that **Satan tests too**. He will bring out the **worst** in us anyway he can. The **choice** is ours, but here is the important point:

*"When God tests **us** we cannot in return **test Him** by our attitude and words. To test and tempt God means to **deliberately** adopt a disobedient posture **and dare Him to do anything about it."*   **Warren Wiersbe**

God Commands–We Obey

In Leviticus, there are some great examples of God **giving His authority** to His people. When God commanded Moses regarding how priests were to represent Him (God) to the people, He gave Moses exact orders. That way, nothing was left to **chance** or the **imagination.**

*"Think about **the church today**. Instead of substituting **people's ideas, religious novelties, fads and entertainment** for **God's Word** and the **songs of Zion**, the first thing the spiritual leaders should ask is, "For what do **the scriptures say?"*   **Warren Wiersbe**

"If" is a Very Big Word

Staying in Leviticus, there are more great lessons about the little word "if". These excerpts come from **Chapter 26**: *"If you walk in my statutes (vs.3); But if you do not obey me (vs.14); but if they confess their iniquity (vs.40)."* As you can see, **if** carries a lot of weight.

> *"Now, in our relationship with God, if I am not walking with Him I had better change directions because He is not going to change His. It's as simple as Amos 3:3, "How can two walk together unless they both agree?"*
> **Warren Wiersbe**

Feel Guilty? Good!

Today, we live in a world that **doesn't have** a lot of guilt, and that is sad. **Warren Wiersbe** wrote this Bible truth:

> *"It's a basic spiritual principal that until people experience the guilt of conviction, they can't enjoy the glory of conversion."*

Be Real–Not Counterfeit

There are **many reasons** why people turn to God. One reason is **not** to make you wealthy, and here is why, as stated by **F. B. Myers**:

> *"If God promised His servants an unbroken run of prosperity, there would be many counterfeit Christians."*

Just Batten down the Hatches

Sometimes trouble just seems to find us, doesn't it? I thought this was a good idea to keep in mind when it does…

*"When the high seas **rage,** it's no time to **change ships."***
Unknown

Anonymous People

Oft times you see **something interesting or noteworthy** signed, "Anonymous". This is also true of some people written about in **the Bible.**

Examples: *Who was **the lad** who supplied the two fishes and loaves of bread? What were the names of **the men** who lowered Paul down the Damascus wall? Who was **the servant girl** who told Naaman to see the prophet so he could be healed? **The answer** is- we **don't know** and it **doesn't matter!*** **Warren Wiersbe** tells us why:

*"As great doors can swing on **small hinges,** so great events can turn upon the deeds of **"small"** and sometimes **"anonymous people."***

Leaders Need to Lead

If we **both love and fear** the Lord, we will be **faithful** to do the work He has called us to do. When spiritual leaders fear **people** instead of fearing **God,** they end up **getting trapped** and that can only lead to failure. **Dr. Bob Jones Sr.** said this about Christian service:

*"The greatest **ability** is **dependability."***

Once Forgiven - Let it go

The Bible clearly says that **God hates sin**. Hebrews 1:9 says, *"You (speaking of God) have **loved** righteousness and **hated** lawlessness."*

*"Sin and the Law **convict** us. But God is a God of **order,** and sin is no exception, so the order here is: **conviction, cleansing, and then celebration**, for the same Word that **wounds** also **heals**. It is as wrong to mourn when God **has forgiven** us as it is to rejoice when sin has **conquered us.** Christians **must believe** what God says about forgiveness and **act upon it.**"*   **Unknown**

Giving and Receiving

The thought of **giving to others** runs deep throughout the Scriptures. Jesus spoke of it often so perhaps it is one of the **secrets** of staying alive and fresh in the Christian life. Here is how someone explains it:

*"If all we ever do **is receive**, we become **reservoirs**, and the waters become **stale and polluted.**"*

Outlook Determines Outcome

How we look at **situations and challenges** of life will often be determined by **where** we look.

*"**When** we look to **the Lord** and His guidance, we **know** that the outcome is in His hands and that assures us we have **nothing to fear.**"*   **Unknown**

Don't Explain, Just Accept

When I was teaching, I came across this little thought–

*"If you **can explain** what's going on in your ministry, **God didn't** do it."*   **Dr. Robert Cook**

Doubt verses Unbelief

There is **a big difference** between doubt and unbelief. We all pass through **the valley of doubt**, and we are not alone. Think of the great names in the Bible who **struggled with doubt: Job, Habakkuk, and Thomas for example.** Here is the difference:

*"Doubters may **question** God and even **debate** God but they never **abandon** God. Doubt is sometimes born out of **a troubled mind or broken heart.***

*However, unbelief is **rebellion against God**. Unbelief is a refusal to **accept** what He says and then acts **directly against** His will."*   **Unknown**

The Vine and the Branches

In **John 15**, Jesus calls **Himself** the Vine and tells us how **we,** as the branches, must abide in Him:

*"The reason being that, if we do so, we will have: prayer **effectual** (vs.7), joy **celestial** (vs. 11), and fruit **perpetual** (vs. 16)."*   **Unknown**

A Wedding of Cana Thought

Jesus' first miracle as recorded in **John 2** is a great story and a reflection of how many people today live their lives here on earth. Someone made this comment:

> *"The **initial wine** offered to the guests is like the world and the **young** who empty their lives in pleasure and there is nothing but **dregs in old age.***
>
> *The Christian life is just **the opposite**. Christ gets **better** as the best wine is kept till last. **The feast follows the fast.**"*

Feeding the Five Thousand

Again in **John's Gospel** is another precious truth we can savor.

In **6:11** we read, *"And Jesus took **the loaves,** and when He had given thanks He distributed them to all **the disciples,** and the disciples to **those sitting down;** and likewise the **fish,** as much as they wanted."* This gives us a picture of–

1. ***A perishing world***
2. ***The powerless disciples***
3. ***The Perfect Savior***

*We, as a perishing world do **what we can do** (find the loaves and fishes), **find helpers** to do what they can do (seat the people and distribute the bounty), and **the Lord will do** what **we cannot do** (perform the miracle only God **could** do).*

Remembering King David

So often when people think of David, they immediately go to his **defeats,** such as his sin with **Bathsheba,** the **murder** of her husband, and his **disobedience to God** by numbering the people when God told him no. David was so much more, listen to what Warren Wiersbe wrote–

*David was a unique blend of **soldier and shepherd, musician and military tactician, commander and commoner.** But the **most important** fact of his life and memory is that **Jesus was never ashamed to call Himself the Son of David.***

Senior Citizen Workers

Many seniors think that because of their age they may have **lost too much** to be of much use to God. Not so. Consider **Eli, the priest in Samuel 1** who raised young Samuel in the house of the Lord and Samuel became one of God's great spokesman and **last of the Judges.**

Someone said, *"Blessed are those **older saints** who help the **new generation** know God and how to live for Him."*

"I Have Sinned"

God makes it clear that He **wants repentance** from us whenever we sin. There are cases in scripture where men have uttered "I have sinned" and they were **either insincere** or wanted to **escape** a bad situation.

*For instance, **King Saul** used it three times but didn't mean it, **Pharaoh** said it to Moses to buy time, **Balaam said it** to the Angel of the Lord after he had beaten his poor donkey, **Achan** said it to Joshua after his sin had cost many lives, **Shimei** cried out to David after Shimei had insulted David as David fled Jerusalem, and of course **the ultimate cry of fear** was "I have sinned by betraying **innocent blood"** (Matt. 27:4) spoken **by Judas Iscariot.***

Necessary Commands to Please God

When Moses told the people what God **expected of them** before they possessed the Promised Land, it boiled down to five words: **fear, walk, love, serve, and keep** (Deut. 10:12, 13).

*"As Christians, we too must walk and serve **in balance. Our list reads as follows: faith and works, character and conduct, worship and service, solitude and fellowship,** and separation **from** the world and ministry and witness **to** the world."*   **Unknown**

Sincerity Always Pleases God?

So many people today, especially in liberal churches, say that **as long as one is sincere**, God will bless them. Not true.

The Bible story in **Deut. 12** tells us how God put the sword in the hands of Israel to **destroy** the pagan Canaanites. Why? Because *the Canaanites would **sacrifice their own children** in the temple fires as a **gift to their god**. Now, who can be **more sincere** than that?*

Peat and Repeat

Time after time, **Moses reminds Israel** of the Covenant between them and the Lord. **Repetition** concerning the things of God is good.

As **Warren Wiersbe** comments, *"Too often God's people **forget** what they **ought to remember** and **remember** what they **ought to forget.**"*

Godly Leaders or Political Liars

In this age of anything goes to be elected, men and women say whatever will **tickle the ears** of voters. They may **fool us,** but God knows every man's **true character**. I'd love to have this thought sent to **every elected person** in Washington D.C., **including the president…**

Psalms 11:4 says, *"He observes the sons of men; **His eyes** examine them…"* to which **Matthew Henry** added this: *"God not only **sees** them but He **sees through** them, not only **knows all they say and do,** but what they **think**, what they **intend,** and even what they **pretend.**"*

The Obituary of Abraham

The Bible has a wonderful **tribute to** "father Abraham." It says he died **"full of years."**

"*It is sad to meet many elderly people today who fail to see* ***the joy of old age.*** *They do not want to share their **old age wisdom** with the younger generation and even as believers are not prepared to meet God in joyful confidence. When they **look back** it is with regret; when they **look ahead** it is with fear; and when they **look around** it is with complaint. Somewhere along the way **they missed** being "full of years.*" **Warren Wiersbe**

Christians Who Downplay Themselves

This is a long title, but the message is short and simple, **don't underestimate your importance** if you are **a child of the King**.

"*Remember, our Lord Jesus Christ **thought highly enough of you to give Himself for you in death and sacrifice.***"
Unknown

Really Bright People

How many times have you met someone really bright–and **they knew it.**

Job was such a man. His story, as told in the Bible, is one of the great pieces of wisdom literature. But **the thought here** is that, in **Chapter 38**, when Job gets to **question God**, Job finds out how smart he really is. The bottom line:

"*Knowledge of **our own ignorance** is the first step **towards wisdom.***"
Unknown

Time and Overtime for God

Proverbs 13:4 talks about time spent **with** or **for** God; *"the soul of **the diligent** shall be made rich."*

Here are a few examples of people who had the gumption to stick to a project:

*"**Adam Clark** spent 40 years on his commentary; **Noah Webster**, 36 years on his dictionary; **the poet Milton** arose at 4 AM to write; **Gibbon** spent 26 years writing The Rise and Fall of the Roman Empire. So man, and **especially the Christian**, when being diligent in the Lord's work, can **find true happiness."*   **Unknown**

God's Still Small Voice

This is one of **my favorite stories** in all the Bible because its message is so needed today in **our lives and churches.**

In **1 Kings 19:12**, Elijah was hiding in a cave when God wanted to get his attention. God showed Elijah His mighty power in **the wind, the earthquake, and the fire,** but Elijah still remained hidden in the cave. It was only when God **spoke to Elijah** in His **still small voice** that Elijah came out from hiding and **listened.** The point is this:

*"In this age of loud music, clapping, and shouting, when it comes to worship, I still **prefer** to listen to God's **still small voice."***   **Warren Wiersbe**

Forgiveness for All?

As humans we sometimes look at **really bad, evil people** and wonder if God would listen if they were to repent.

According to the Bible, **God does,** and that is that. Good example is **Manasseh,** one of the worst rulers of Judah. **Hezekiah,** his father, had turned Judah back to God but Manasseh reversed all the good his father had done: Manasseh was **the worst of the worst.**

Yet scripture says Manasseh **humbled himself, repented,** God heard him and forgave him, and all was new (2 Chron. 33:11).

   Amazing grace and unbelievable mercy from our awesome God.

God's Way or the People's Way

Sometimes even **good, godly people** attempt to serve God, but want to do it **their way** instead of what God has said or commanded.

The perfect example is **David,** who was caught up in the excitement of moving the **Ark of the Covenant** to Jerusalem. God had clearly instructed Moses to **have rings put on the Ark** so it could be carried by men with poles. But David had it loaded onto a **new cart** which nearly dumped the Ark, and the result was the death of the man who tried to keep it from hitting the ground. David **was angry with God** because of this tragedy, but it was really David's fault due to his lack of planning before moving the Ark.

Sound familiar? *How many times do you remember personally, if you **had done things God's way,** as outlined in the Old or New Testaments, the **results** would have been different?*

Wasted Opportunities

How many times have we **missed or wasted** opportunities to serve the Lord?

Warren Wiersbe hit the nail on the head when he gave this **thought for today**:

*"Opportunity doesn't **shout, it whispers**, and our ears must be attentive. Opportunity **knocks**, it doesn't **knock down the door**, which we better be alert to open. To ignore God given opportunity is to **waste the past, jeopardize the future, and frustrate the present.**"*

Ezra Led by Example

Ezra was an unbelievable **leader.** Called to lead the people back to Jerusalem **after the 70 years in captivity,** he made a crucial decision. First, he **became a man of prayer.** He prepared his heart to *"**seek** the Law of the Lord, and to **do it,** and **teach** its statutes and ordinances in Israel."* His heart **was set to obey** God's Law.

Here's the point of the lesson, so well put by **Warren Wiersbe**:

*"It's in the **obeying** of the Word that we experience the blessings, **not** in the **reading, hearing, or what one thinks** he already **knows.** No, one is blessed in what one **does.** If our knowledge of the truth **doesn't result in obedience,** then we wind up with a **big head,** instead of a **burning heart.** God's truths become **a toy** to play with instead of **a tool** to build with."*

God's Patience

When you study the **Old Testament books** outlining the struggles between the divided kingdoms of **Israel and Judah,** one theme comes through time and again: the **patience of God.**

Why God left **a man like Ahaz** in power for **22 years** is beyond me. Ahaz influenced **whole generations towards evil**; why did God not **strike him down** or remove him?

Honestly, **I don't know.** But *I do know He has had the same patience **with me.***

My Enemies

I found this little jewel someplace:

> *"**Whatever** keeps me from **my Bible** is my enemy. **Whatever** keeps me from **mediating on God** injures my soul."*
>
> **Unknown**

This Scared World

Listen to what **A. W. Tozer** had to say about fear among Christians–

> *"There are **a lot** of scared people out there. It's understandable, but a fear-ridden Christian needs **to examine** his or her defense. Bible believing Christians should be the **last people** on earth to give way to hysteria. If you **know** you are in God's hand, talk and act like it! We can **never convince** a scared world there is **peace and assurance** at the foot of the cross if we act upon our fears **the same** as those who make no profession of Christ."*

The Ark of the Covenant and Jesus

Somewhere in my Old Testament studies came **this thought** from some wise person:

*"What the Ark was to **ancient Israel**, Jesus Christ is to **God's people today**. So, when He is given His rightful **place of preeminence** in our lives, He will **bless us** and work on our behalf. God still gives **His best** to those who leave the choice **to Him**. When Jesus is Lord, the **future** is your friend and you can walk through **each day** confident of **His presence** and **His help**."*

Successful Christians

Why wouldn't men and women **working for the Lord** want to be just as **successful** as any other individual? **The key** is making sure good old **Mr. Pride** doesn't spoil you or **Mr. Satan** doesn't defeat you. **Someone** supplied these three questions every worker for the Lord should ask themselves:

1. Did I **obey** the will of God?
2. Was I **empowered** by the Spirit of God?
3. Did I **serve** to the glory of God?

If I can answer **"yes"** to all of these questions, then my **ministry will succeed** in God's eyes, no matter what people may think, or say, or do.

Who Am I?

I put this entry in the **personal** section because it asks one of the most **important questions** mortal man can ask God–**who am I?** Look at these men, who **when picked by God** to lead His people believed themselves **inadequate** for the task.

When God told him to lead the people out of Egypt, Moses said, **"Who am I?"** (Exodus 3:11). Likewise **David,** when told he would be the vehicle by whom God **would send Messiah** said, **"Who am I?"**(1 Chron. 29:14). Even **Saul,** in an act of humbleness upon learning he would be **Israel's first king** said, **"Who am I?"**(1 Sam. 18:18).

So, when I first heard **this song, "Who Am I"**, written **by Rusty Goodman of the Goodman Family Singers**, it was love from the beginning. Just read **the words** of the song and if they don't stir your blood, brother, you should pray about it:

*"Oh when **I think** about of how He **left His home** in glory,*
Came and dwelt** among **the lowly such as I,

*To **suffer shame** and **such disgrace**, on Mt. Calvary **take my place,***
***Then I ask myself** a question–who am I?*

***Who am I** that **a King** would **bleed and die** for?*
***Who am I,** that He would pray, "not **my will,** thine" for?*

The answer** I may **never** know, why He **ever loved me so,
*That **to an old rugged cross** He'd go–for **who am I?"***

The Apostle **Paul** put it so well:

Romans 5:6-8 *"For when we were **still without strength**, in due time Christ died **for the ungodly**. For scarcely for **a righteous man** will one die; yet **perhaps** for a good man someone would even **dare to die.** But God demonstrates **His own love towards us,** in that **while we were still sinners, Christ died for us."***

CHAPTER EIGHT

The Love, Grace, and Will of God

For **mere men** like you and I to explain to others about God's love, grace, and will demands a **higher plane** than this writer is capable. Great men of God have written **complete books** on these subjects, so I would be foolish to steal **a piece here or a piece there** and say this is what **I believe** is meant by God's attributes of love, grace, and will.

Simply put, I believe God's love has to **be felt,** His grace **experienced,** and His will **accepted.** Hopefully, in heaven, there will be **classes taught** by the Master on these subjects because there is so much **misunderstanding** and **over simplification** of the true meaning within the dynamics of the relationship between God and man.

However, **what I can offer** are the following thoughts and illustrations devoted to these three virtues: the love, grace, and will of God. This will be a nice detour **away from the subjects** of this book dealing with issues of **sin, warnings, and judgment.** So drop off your baggage, empty your head of guilt, and **let's rejoice** in some of these pearls about the **love, grace, and the will of God.**

Class 101 in Heaven

Mentioned in the chapter introduction, was the fact that we will **learn from the Master** when we get to glory. Here is a thought I found on that very subject:

> *"Heaven will be our **school**. God will be our **teacher**. His grace will be the **subject**. We will be the **students**, and the school term will be **eternity**."* **Unknown**

When Circumstances Seem Unsurmountable

We all have had those moments when everything is **out of control**. As Christians we have a **secret weapon**. Here it is:

> *"**Peace** is the unruffled quietness which defies the crashing, crushing circumstances of life. **Grace is** the **cause**, and peace the effect."* **Unknown**

Grace and Love Combined

Here are three profound thoughts taken from the writings of a past voice for God, **Donald Grey Barnhouse** (1895-1960).

*Love that reaches **up is adoration.***

*Love that reaches **across is affection**.*

*Love that reaches **down is grace.***

How to Display God's Grace

I don't remember where this thought came from, but there is **good, solid** Christian truth in it:

> *"The **difference** between **patience and longsuffering** is the difference between **enduring without complaint** and **enduring without retaliation**. Believers display **God's grace** when they suffer **patiently** and praise the Lord in **the midst of trials.**"*

God's Will Revealed

Many times **we pray for God's will,** and then act surprised when **His answer** is **positive.** This thought may help:

> *"God does not reveal His will to us in order to **satisfy our curiosity,** nor to **cater to our ambitions or pride,** but rather in order that we might **please Him** in all that we do."*   **Unknown**

The Purpose of the Law

There is a lot to study and learn about the doctrines of **law and grace.** Later on in this chapter, I have a complete dissertation from the **study of Galatians.** In the meantime, think about this:

> *"Whereas **the law** has **a curse** for those who **fail to keep it,** the **gospel of grace** has **a curse** for those who seek to **change it.** The **law's purpose?** Paul tells us in **Galatians 3:19,** "Till the Seed shall come."*   **Unknown**

More Grace Needed

Here is a quick reminder for all of us **"senior saints"**–

*"To grow old **gracefully** calls for **more grace** than nature can provide."*

Love Makes Other Things Work

It is amazing how things seem **to go better** when we have the **love for God** in our lives, as in the following thought:

*"**Love is** the oil that makes the wheels of **obedience** run."*
Unknown

Greetings with a Meaning

When mentor **Paul** was training young **Timothy** for the ministry he often used **his greetings** for all types of **teaching**. Probably **some preacher** wrote this:

*For instance, when he wished Timothy **"grace, mercy, and peace"** he was really saying: grace to the **worthless**, mercy to the **helpless**, and peace to the **restless**.*

Make the Right Choice

There are examples of **connections** in the Bible that require actions of man **to** God; and that involves both **free choice and free will**. God's **will** would be that we **follow Him**, but that is where man's **free choice** enters the equation. Look at it this way:

*"If there are **a thousand steps** between us and God, **He** will take **all but one**. He will leave that **final one** for us. The choice is ours."*
Max Lucado

Jesus Our Servant?

Catherine Marshall wrote this amazing revelation to use in a class I was teaching about **God's love for His flock.** Think back to **John 13** and the Last Supper and ponder this:

"Jesus wrapped **a towel** around His waist, poured **water** into a basin and began **to wash the disciple's feet**, (including **Judas**). **Peter** objected that this was beneath the dignity of the Master. But **Jesus insisted** and said, *"If I do not wash you, you have no part in me."*

Let this **sink in:**

*"unless I can believe in this much **love for me, unless** I can and will accept Him with faith as **my servant** as well as **my God, unless** I truly know that it's **my** good He seeks, **not** His glory.....then I **cannot** have His **companionship."**

Bullets for Building

The bullets I refer to here **are words.** The words (bullets) are **grace, mercy, and peace.** Now let's put them to work–

*"In our walk with Christ we need grace for **every service,** mercy for **every failure,** and peace for **every circumstance."**

Unknown

When God Reveals Himself to Man

Here is a thought that came from someone who we may refer to as a "deeper life believer":

> "God can reveal Himself to whoever and whenever **He wills.** However, only those who are truly **ready to meet Him** will be able to **find Him.** He won't reveal Himself to superficial followers who are looking for a **"new experience"** they can brag about, or to curious Christians who want to **"sample"** a deeper fellowship with God. No, God **longs** to reveal Himself to us, **but** we are the ones who make it difficult."

Jonah and God's Will

We're all familiar with the **story of Jonah**, still a classic for the ages. But here is some thought provoking information about the story:

> "The **will of God** will never lead you where the **grace of God** can't keep you and the **power of God** can't use you. Our **perfect example** is Jonah. Sent to that **"great city" Nineveh,** this Hebrew prophet converted perhaps **600,000 souls** to the fear of Jehovah."

Great Character for God

Here is a wonderful truth that came from **Chuck Swindoll's** book, **"The Darkness and the Dawn"**. **I highly recommend** you read this during the Easter season, it is a powerful, thought provoking book on the crucifixion-

> *"God's great lessons are often taught on an anvil of **pain, illness, and mistreatment**. But here is where **great character** is forged and building blocks shaped for the spiritual life. We **learn this best**, all of us, on **the same level:** at the **foot of the cross**. It's there, in the **dark shadow of Jesus' suffering and sacrifice** that we learn best."*

Grace and Heaven

On a lesson about grace, this comment by **Mark Twain**, though nonbiblical, probably applies to a lot of cranky folks:

> *"Heaven goes **by favor**. If it went **by merit**, you would stay out, and **your dog** would go in."*

Love or Lust

Many Christians, especially the young, **confuse love with lust** or vice-versa. Paul made it clear to the saints in **1 Thessalonians 4:3,** that *"you abstain from sexual immorality."*

I found this thought from **Josh McDowell:**

> *"Love can **wait** to give; it is lust that **can't wait** to get."*

The Redeemed and Secured Believer's Poem

When we think of the promises that **awaits true believers,**
this little ditty says it all:

> *There is no condemnation,*
>
> *There is **no hell for me,***
>
> *The torture and the fire,*
>
> *My eyes shall **never see;***
>
> *For me there is no sentence,*
>
> *For me there is **no sting,***
>
> *Because the Lord who loves me,*
>
> *Shall **shield me with His wing.***

Paul Gerhardt

Tough Love

Hebrews 12:6 says, *"The Lord **disciplines** the ones He loves."* **Focus on the Family** founder, **James Dobson,** had this thought:

> *"Genuine love **demands toughness** in moments of crisis."*

Love Sent the Servant

There is a tremendous truth in **John 20:21** when Jesus said to His disciples, *"**Peace to you.** As the Father has sent me, I **also send you.**"*

As believers, we are **not** to be selfish with His given **joy of peace** but are to share it with others. Someone wrote, *"As He **sends us,** remember how **He was sent;** as a **poor** person, as a **servant** to serve, how He **emptied Himself** of all for all, how **He delighted** to do His Fathers will, and **in all these things His goal was still the cross.**"* Repeating what He said, *"I also send you."*

Obeying the Will of God

Many people ask the question, "How will **I know** when it is the will of God?" Good question. Consider this thought for today:

> *"To assist us we have the Holy Spirit **within,** the Word of God **before** us, and the interceding Savior **above** us. We will know **if** we stay tuned in."*   **Unknown**

Darkness and Light

The stories **from Exodus** about how God continually kept His people Israel aware of His **presence and protection** are comforting. Remember how Moses wrote about the pillar of **cloud** in the day and the pillar of **fire** at night? It was **light** to the Hebrews but **darkness** to their enemies. **Someone** made this great comparison–

> *"It is like the Word of God to us today. Unbelievers are blind to the Word and **cannot see** its truths. When we believe and **accept the will of God** through Christ–we move **from** darkness **into** light."*

God Will Not Break a Covenant

There is an interesting truth in **Deut. 2** that puts a different light on **the Jewish–Arab conflict**. I truly **believe** the Bible teaches that–

> *God's **love** for His children Israel and His **oath** to keep and protect them He has always **upheld** in spite of their sin and idolatry. But God also had **a covenant with Ishmael and Esau.** He would not give the Jews any of **their land** He had promised to the **sons of Hagar.** Remember, God had **promised** He would "**make them (the Arab nation) a great nation,"** which He has.*

Which Way Will You Go?

Here is a **short three part question** someone wrote pertaining to the **will of God.**

> *"There are cases where God makes it very clear **what His will is.** The question is, will you **obey** it, **ignore** it, or **resist** it?"*

The Law and Grace

A **former student** of mine gave me the following information many years ago.

Old Testament law and **New Testament grace** are an **interesting yet puzzling** study but **both** are part of the truth of God. Read **slowly and think** about each comparison–

*Law is **prohibiting and requiring**; grace is God **beseeching and bestowing.** Law is a ministry of **condemnation;** grace, of **forgiveness.** Law **curses;** grace **redeems** the curse. Law **kills;** grace **makes alive.** Law **shuts every mouth** before God; grace **opens every mouth** to praise Him. Law puts a great and guilty **distance** between man and God; grace makes guilty man **nigh** before God. Law says "**Hate** thine enemy;" grace says "**Love your enemies,** bless them that despitefully use you." Law says, **do and live;** grace says, **believe** and live. Law **utterly condemns** the best man; grace **freely justifies** the worst. Law **stones** the adulteress; grace says, "Neither do I **condemn** thee; go, and sin no more." Under law the **sheep die** for the shepherds; under grace the **Shepherd dies** for the sheep.*

*Everywhere the Scriptures present law and grace in **sharply contrasted** spheres. The **mingling** of them in much of the **current teaching** of the day **spoils both,** for law is **robbed of its terror,** and grace of **its freeness.***

C. I. Scofield

Sin and Grace

Here is another comparison, this time **using men** of the Bible as examples:

In **Chapter 16 of Judges,** the Spirit leaves **Samson** because of his great sins with **Delilah. King Saul** also lost his crown due to numerous sins.

> **Warren Wiersbe** had this comment, *"Sin **makes slaves** out of kings; grace **makes kings** out of sinners."*

God's Grace to the Gentiles

Can you recall the **first resurrection** in the Bible? It was **The Widow of Zarephate** incident recorded in **1 Kings 17:17-24**: look it up.

When **Jesus recounted this story** to His own people in **Nazareth of Galilee,** that God is a God of **all** people, including the Gentiles and not just **His chosen,** they wanted **to kill Him.**

Remember this the next time you think, *"**Woe is me...**" that we Gentiles are a **blessed people** to be **included** in God's plan.*

Grace and the Cross

In the **Book of Job**, all three of his friends pounded him about their convictions that **Job was suffering** because of something **wrong in his life**. No grace from them, that's for sure.

However, along **with** grace, God wants us to **stand straight and tall** when **His** honor is on the line. This is a good thought about **modern religion:**

> *"Many look for an **easy** religion; easy to **understand**, easy to **follow**, a religion with **no mystery**, no insolvable **problems or snags**, an **escape** for every trial, and one where **God spares** all **strife, suffering, and doubt**. In short, a religion **without the cross**. That cannot be, because true Christianity **demands** that we **give honor and reverence to the cross."***   **Unknown**

Grace for the Wounded

I remember the **first time** I ever heard this quote. I was working with a salesman friend who was a Christian, and we were discussing how **"church people"** can be so ruthless when it comes to judging someone in the flock who had sinned.

You may have heard this but it bears repeating. My friend said to me, *"You know, don't you, that the **Christian Army** is the only army that **shoots it's wounded."***

Some Thoughts on Love

Here are a couple jewels I saved by **Warren Wiersbe** and his comments concerning **1 John 4,** that great love chapter:

> *"We are **not saved** by loving Christ; we **are saved** by believing on Christ."*

> *"It is important that Christians **show progress** in their understanding of love. To love one another simply out of a **sense of duty** is good, but to love out **of appreciation** (rather than obligation) is even **better."***

And this final thought kind of sums up the whole chapter, *"True **spiritual** experience involves the whole man. The **mind** must understand spiritual truths; the **heart** must love and appreciate it, and the **will** must act upon it."*

PERSONAL REFLECTION

Defining Moments from Israel

In **your walk** with the Lord, hopefully you have had those **special occasions** when **you knew** God was very present: times when **your soul** was alive and awakened **to the Holy Spirit.** It cannot always be **explained** or even **understood,** but it is definitely **felt.**

I would like to recall a couple **of personal experiences** for you. Please understand it is **not about me,** it is just **to explain** that if we open **our hearts** to God, He is always there for **us.** The interesting part is that these episodes **happened in Israel.** That makes them all the more unique and unforgettable.

In 2003, I made my first trip to Israel. The **main purpose** was as a volunteer on an **archaeological dig at Kursie.** This was an ancient village on the **Sea of Galilee** where the "Miracle of the Swine" event took place as described in **Mark, Chapter 5.**

Since we had the **weekends off,** a group of us decided to hire a bus to take us to **Jerusalem** and tour the city.

One of the **"defining moments"** came when I entered Jerusalem, that eternal city, **for the first time.** I can only describe **the "feel" of history**, like slipping back into Biblical times, and that feeling seemed to cover me like a blanket. Remembering Jerusalem's past, beginning with **King**

David, the ancient **prophets,** the rebuilding of the wall by **Nehemiah, Herod's Temple, Jesus'** many visits, people like **Paul, Peter, the Romans, the Crusaders, the 6 Day War:** the thoughts went on and on. To see the places where these things happened, **plus** the **sounds, the smells, and the people** in their **ethnic** dress representing **their heritage** or **their religion,** confirmed that what **I felt** was the Bible, God's Word, **alive** and solidified.

The next "**moment**" was completely **unexpected.**

We visited the **Western Wall** of Herod's Temple, also known as **The Wailing Wall,** because for centuries Jews have **cried out** to God to send **the Messiah** and return them to their righteous place **before all the peoples** of the world. On **this particular day,** I simply wanted to **touch and pray** at the wall. Gentiles **are allowed** at the wall as long **as their heads are covered:** there are **free paper yarmulkes** available. I must confess that I felt **a sense of awe and reverence** as I approached this **holy spot.** What happened next **can only be described** as divine because when I placed both of **my hands** and my **forehead** against the wall it felt as if some **low voltage** current was **passing through my body.** I have **no doubt whatsoever** that this was the **Holy Spirit.** All I could think about were the **millions upon millions** of **prayers of God's people,** the Jews, and how their prayers had completely **saturated** this spot. God was simply **allowing me to share** in the blessing. All I could do was stand **still,** be **quiet,** and think, "**Holy, holy, holy**". Truly a "**defining moment**" never to be forgotten.

PART FOUR

*Daily Trials
and Tribulations*

CHAPTER NINE

Personal Battles and Satanic Wars

As a blood bought Christian, I have a positive outlook, I **am not** a negative person. I wish this book had more chapters devoted to **happy** thoughts and **love** related stories. However, as I started to separate the material gathered over the years in conjunction with my teaching, the final results spoke for themselves.

There are, as you will find throughout this book**, many things** pertaining to and commenting on **the love of God**. God's nature **is love,** but His judgment is **against sin.** From Adam to this very day, man and his downfall have **hi-jacked the scriptures** and caused these spiritual battles.

Strong **teaching** sometimes begets **strong reaction.** Teachers sometimes step on people's toes (including their own), and they don't like it. However, I found a good place **to hide** if a truth wounded someone: **I hid behind Jesus. I know** that as long as I stick to what **He said** in scripture I cannot rightly be condemned or accused. After all, He went toe to toe with some of **the nastiest people** on the planet when He was here **and never lost** a battle nor ever retracted a statement or accusation. Now that's my kind of Leader, and if folks accuse me of being hurtful, **I'll err on His side** every time.

So, if you enjoy a **good scrap** or just some bullets to **fire back** at the enemies of Christ, here are some good **"Thoughts for Today."** If some seem too strong, **I'm O.K.** with that. If you want to **complain,** you'll find me **hiding** behind The Man with the "whip of cords" **(John 2:15).**

Sins of Self

I didn't write this but **I wish I had,** because we all know someone who we are **afraid** to ask, "How are you today?" for obvious reasons. Here is the quote:

*"Christians who **dwell** on their sickness and operations **hurt** their fellowship with others. Too often, it is but a **manifestation** of one of the **hyphenated sins** of self-life: self-pity, self-occupation, and self-display."* **Unknown**

Spiritual Whining

This is a good follow up because it is one of the **few places** in the Bible where God calls out someone **by name.** In Jeremiah 45, **Baruch** is warned of **self-seeking sympathy** just because he is discouraged. Look it up, it's good medicine. Here's a suggestion:

*"We **Christians** need to learn the **same lesson.** How can we complain when we **possess** so great a salvation? We cannot **collapse** under every test. Let God be God, **in control,** and **stop whining** at **every bump** in the road"* **Unknown**

Trials Defined

I must have been working on a lesson **concerning trials of life** because these two were side by side in my notes. Here is some good **food for thought,** listen:

> *"God **permits trials** so He can build **Godly character.** Character doesn't **automatically** come from reading books and attending church, it also involves **bearing burdens, fighting battles, and even feeling pain."***
>
> **Charles Swindoll**

Society's Laws and the Christian

This may be the **next battleground** for Christianity.

Today, legislators, congress, judges, lawyers, and activist do-gooders are all striving to **pass laws** thinking it will **make "good people"** and a **"good society,"** but what we are **seeing** is that not everything that's legally passed is **moral** and **biblical.**

The greater wrong is this: *some human activities that **our courts** now sanction and **society defends,** God someday will **judge as abominable sin.***

"The Lord is a Man of War"

The above is a **direct quote of Exodus 15:3**. Look it up.

God was preparing His people as they were about to enter the **Promised Land** where many enemies awaited. Today, many folks are disturbed by the **violence in the Bible** (even some Christians) but Satan made it that way, not the Lord! Here is what someone said–

> *"The Christian life is a **battleground, not a playground** and there are enemies to **fight** and territories **to gain for the Lord**. Also, the **Book of Revelation** tells us all about the end times and praise the Lord that as Christians we will be on **the winning side** of the battle between **The King of Kings and Satan."***   **Unknown**

Powerful Poison

The **Book of Esther** is a story with a lot of twists and turns: good versus evil and historical values.

One of the interesting aspects is the reaction of **King Artaxerxes** when he is defied by **Queen Vashti** in Chapter 1. **Warren Wiersbe** made this observation:

> *"When **the ego is pricked,** it releases a **powerful poison** that makes people do all sorts of things they'd never do if they were **humble** and **submitted** to the Lord."*

When Problems Come

We must **keep in mind** that problems and tests come in all forms and varieties. So, Christian:

*"When the world seems **against you**–remember: God examines with **tests,** the devil with **temptations,** and the world with **persecutions.**"*   **Unknown**

Watch What You Conform To

Psalm 115 is a great **comparison** between the God of the Bible and the god of **man's making**. This makes the unsaved **behave** like the gods they **worship**.

When we bring this thought into **the church age**, **Warren Wiersbe** offers this warning:

*"In every age, there is the tremendous pressure to **conform to** "**popular religion**" and to **abandon** the fundamentals of the faith. Satan's **counterfeit religion** is subtle, requiring **spiritual discernment** to recognize."*

Mean as a Skunk

Here's a **true story** that may make you smile.

One Sunday when I was teaching Adult Bible Study at First Baptist of Sarasota, Florida, the lesson was about **Adam and fallen man**. The class discussion drifted into examples of people class members had met that were **mean and ugly** their whole lives.

I'll never forget **Billy Murphy's** contribution about a man from his hometown in Ohio. This fellow was so nasty, Billy claims that *"when **he died,** the **nicest thing** people could say about him was that he made **a nice corpse.**"*

The Sins of Babylon

We Americans have **not learned** the lessons of the past as we roll along **deeper and deeper** into sinfulness. As **Warren Wiersbe** wrote about **Israel** picking up the **sins of Babylon:**

*"First they **accepted** their sinful ways, then **approved** of them, and finally **enjoyed them themselves.**"*

Working Together

Here is a good thought for **God's people** to keep in mind as we **face the opposition** of the world every day:

*"Isn't it **sad** that the Lord's people sometimes have **difficulty** working together for **the kingdom,** but the people of the world **have no problems** uniting against **Christian values.**"*   **Unknown**

Ridicule

In the **Book of Nehemiah**, when Nehemiah's enemies had **no other weapo**n to use against him, they used ridicule.

Ridicule, someone has said is: **"the weapon** of those who have no other."** Whether in the **secular** fields of science, research, business, or in **Christian ministry,** just about everyone who has ever **accomplished anything** has faced **ridicule.** Here are a few examples—

"Jesus was ridiculed **by the Pharisees** *and they even went so far as to* **mock Him on the cross.** *On the day of* **Pentecost,** *the newly given Holy Spirit and the speaking in tongues caused the* **Jews** *to say the men* **were drunk.** *The Greek philosophers called Paul a* **"babbler"** *and Festus told Paul he was* **out of his mind.** *But Nehemiah and these other examples* **knew** *that the* **hand of God** *was on them."*

Warren Wiersbe

More Ridicule

Along with ridicule, it has been noted that some people can **stand bravely** when they are being **shot at,** but **collapse** when someone **laughs at them.**

Thomas Carlyle called this type of ridicule *"the language* **of** *the devil."*

Discouragers Cause Discouragements

Before we leave Nehemiah, let's look at another group: **discouragers.** They were the people who tried to stop Nehemiah's work as he rebuilt the wall around Jerusalem. Thanks to **Warren Wiersbe** for these great thoughts–

*"Pressures from without often cause pressures from within by **discouragements** through **compromise**. Nehemiah had **constant pressure** from without the camp.*

*In the **Christian's life**, usually this is an indication of **something wrong** with their spiritual walk. Perhaps they **have lost faith** in **themselves** and the **Word of God** and are primarily interested in their own agenda. The **bottom line** is this: "A double minded person **hinders** the work of the Lord."*

Rejecting God: Jewish Style

I **love and support Israel** for the obvious reason: they are **God's Chosen people,** as He has pointed out numerous times in scripture. However, Israel's **rejection** of God has also been **duly noted** by the writers of the Bible. Here are three examples:

1. *In Samuel 8 they rejected **God the Father** when they asked **for a king.***

2. *The same for **God the Son** in John 19:15 when they cried out, "We have **no king but Caesar."***

3. *And **God the Holy Spirit** when they **stoned Stephen** to death–Acts 7:51.*

Satan's Questions

Have you ever known people thought to be solid Christians and then watch as they completely **fall away** from following the Lord? I have, (myself included), and **this reminder** is food for thought.

*"Using **Adam and Eve** as an example, once Satan had them **questioning** what God said, they were ready to **disobey** His Word, believe Satan's **lies** and the **final** step was to openly rebel against **God's commands.**"*   **Unknown**

Archaeology and its Belief System

I have been **fortunate** to have participated in four archeological digs in Israel, and they have been **great experiences.**

The one thing that has been troubling though, has been the **opinions** of the **archaeologist in charge.** These seemingly intelligent men and women **rarely if ever** refer to **the Bible** as a source when explaining the **evidence** of something that was **uncovered** at the site. They always quote another archaeologist **or someone** who wrote **something** about a dig site **instead** of **The One** who put everything there in the first place, **God Himself.**

Evil in the World

The question is often asked: **Why** does God permit evil in the world? **Not an easy question** to answer to **a non-Christian,** but I do **offer the following to believers–**

First, **our ways** are not **His ways.** He permits men to make their own **choices** and in His sovereign **will or purposes,** He does **not** make mistakes. **Abraham** asked: *"Shall not the Judge of the world **do right?"*** Even **backslidden Eli,** when he received all of the bad news about his family, said *"It is **of the Lord,** let Him do what seems **good to Him."***

> *"There are no easy **answers** to settle our minds but there are numerous dependable **promises** to heal our hearts, and **faith** is nurtured **on promises, not explanations."***
>
> **Unknown**

Family Feuds and Disagreements

Of all the problems we face in life, **family disagreements** can be the most painful. Even the Bible records many examples: **Cain and Abel, Jacob and Esau, Joseph and his brothers, David** and his father-in-law **Saul,** and **Paul** tells of family spats in the New Testament churches **at Corinth, Galicia, and Philippi.** Here's a thought:

> *"There are times when avoiding conflict is **cowardly,** but there are other times when it is a sign of **wisdom and courage.** Jesus Himself said, **Blessed** are the peacemakers..."*
>
> **Warren Wiersbe**

The Mixed Multitude

In **Exodus 11,** we read about those who **joined with Israel** when they left Egypt and caused a lot of problems with their complaints. **Warren Wiersbe** had this thought:

> *"Unfortunately, we have the **same situation** in our churches today. As Jesus taught about the **parable of the tares** and Paul the **false brethren** and **false gospel,** the "mixed multitude" are seated **firmly** in our pews."*

Contaminations

Here's **"a thought for today"** someone **wrote** that covers a lot of time and subjects–

> *"Just as **Moses warned** the people about being **curious** about the pagan gods, **Christians** need to be careful about playing with the **poisons** of false doctrines, writings, and teachers."*

The Way, Error, and Doctrine of Balaam

A fascinating study is the **life of Balaam** in the Book of Numbers. It is **an old story,** but it is as **modern as today** because Satan is still using it to **destroy** the Lord's work and churches. Let's look at them one at a time:

1. **The Way of Balaam.** *He had a lifestyle of a soothsayer and false prophet **who used religion** as a way of personal profit. He and his way caused people to **deliberately rebel** against the will of God and **chose money over spiritual values and souls.** He is **in a pulpit** somewhere every Sunday. A good example: **Judas.** Where did **his money** get him?*

2. **The Error of Balaam.** *These are **the cultist** who prey upon **weak people of faith** and lead them astray by **false teaching** about money, power over people, and even through the lies of sexual freedom.*

3. **The Doctrine of Balaam.** *As Balaam used the children of Israel at **the feast of Baal Peor** to just "blend in," so do Christians today want to be **like the world** and all its trappings. We're taught its ok to **be saved** and **live like the unsaved** because God's **grace** gives us **the freedom** to disobey His laws. The truth of the matter is that **any doctrine** that allows sin is a **cancerous growth** and must be removed.*

Now, how does Balaam **creep into the church?** The list is long, and some might not agree, but this is one man's opinion: **compromised preaching, temporal music, weak leadership, accepting the world's standards, and false teachers.** God give us the knowledge **to see Balaam** from afar off.

Battles and Spiritual Wars

I have noted that Moses had to warn the children of Israel many times that, in order to possess and claim the Promised Land, would mean battles and conflicts.

In **these days,** we too have many battles to fight. The **question** is whether the Lord's troops have the stomach for it. Someone **offered this thought:**

> *"You are but a **poor soldier** of Christ if you **think** you can overcome **without fighting,** and suppose you can have **the crown without the conflict.** "*

Seekers and Sneakers

In **Joshua 9,** there is an interesting story of how Joshua **was hood-winked** by the **men of Gibeon** into believing that they were ambassadors of good will, in order to avoid being destroyed. They were liars, but it worked.

We have people doing the **same thing today** in order to sneak into the church. Need proof? Read **2 Peter 2** and the epistle of **Jude.**

Warren Wiersbe, who has served as a pastor for many years, recalls how **"church sneakers"** first give a *"profession of faith,"* then the **sad tales** of woe to break your heart, and then **pick the pocket** of the church. *"Of all liars, **religious liars are the worst.** "*

Songs to God in the Night

Have you ever had a night where **sleep escapes you** no matter what?

I have, and sometimes I try and remember **a favorite spiritual song** to occupy my mind. **Like Paul and Silas** who sang at midnight in **prison** after being beaten, they had no light to see the words but relied on their memories for the **songs of Zion.**

Spurgeon said, *"Songs in the night come **only from God;** they are **not** in the **power of man."***

Spiritual Highs and Lows

Many of us can testify that being a child of the King **does not** get us a free pass when it comes to **problems.** Meditate on these highs and lows from **Warren Wiersbe:**

*"**Jesus** left the glory of the **Mount of Transfiguration** and headed for the **valley of conflict, Paul** left the **heights of heaven** to return to earth along with his **thorn in the flesh,** and **Solomon,** while still soaking in the glory of his **God given wisdom** was asked to **divide a baby."***

Man Made Religions

There are many examples in the Bible, and in this world, of men who sought to be gods or at least gather their own religious following. Here are a couple of examples:

> In the Old Testament, **Jeroboam**, *in order to keep the people from going to Jerusalem to worship, set up his own* **temple**. *He had a golden calf,* **priests** *(him being one), and his own* **festivals and sacrifices.**
>
> *Our modern example today are the* **Jehovah's Witnesses,** *founded by Charles T. Russell, and* **Mormonism,** *founded by Joseph Smith in 1830. Unlike scripture, they* **do not** *see Jesus as God and that is their undoing.*

If He Were Alive Today

I am a real **disciple of A. W. Tozer** (1897-1963). This is **not to say** he **replaces Christ** as my Lord and Savior, but when I read **his writings** and see **his heart for God,** it gives me direction in **my** walk. Listen to what **he wrote in the 1950's** and see if he was on target **with today:**

> *"This is a blasé generation. People have been* **overstimulated** *to the place where their nerves are jaded and their tastes* **corrupted.** *The* **sacred** *has been* **secularized,** *the holy* **vulgarized,** *and* **worship** *is now* **entertainment.** *A dopey, blear-eyed generation constantly* **seeks new excitement,** *thrills for* **worn out sensibilities,** *and invents things of interest to* **replace** *anything common or boring."*

Now I ask you, was he a man **ahead** of his time?

Satan's Tools

Our adversary, the Devil, has a **whole truckload** of weapons to use **against us.** They must be working very well as **the world** is buying them left and right. Satan doesn't **shy away** from Christians, as **we all know.** Here is a list of five things he will attempt to focus your mind upon:

1. **Doubt**
2. **Discouragement**
3. **Diversion**
4. **Defeat**
5. **Delay**

Take a long look at that list. **You know** he has used them against you at some time in your life. Just be ready to **recognize them** when it happens again.

Feel Sorry for Yourself? Read on...

When **Fanny Crosby** (1820-1915) was only six weeks old, a doctor **mistakenly** put hot poultices on her inflamed eyes to treat a common cold. This caused her to **lose her sight.**

However, if you know her history, you know that **God used** this marvelous vessel to write such songs such as "**Safe in the Arms of Jesus**," "**Blessed Assurance**," "**To God be the Glory**," "**A Wonderful Savior is Jesus My Lord**," and countless others. **My point** is this: listen to what she wrote **at the age of 8 years** old:

*"O what a **happy** soul am I, although I cannot see;*

*I am resolved that in this world **contented** I will be.*

*How many **blessings** I enjoy that other people don't;*

*To weep and sigh **because I'm blind**, I cannot and I won't."*

So **the thought here** is: *"When problems won't **go away** or God doesn't remove them, **be submissive.**"*

Before we leave this great woman of faith, this is what **she once said** to a preacher when he **in sorrow,** mentioned her blindness, *"If I had been **given a choice** at birth I would have **asked** to be blind, **because** when I get to heaven, the first face I will see will be the One who died for me."*

CHAPTER TEN

Bits and Pieces–Crumbs from the Master's Table

We Gentiles have much to be **thankful for** when it comes to anything from God.

The Syro-Phoenician woman from the region of Tyre and Sidon is our **perfect example**. She pestered Jesus constantly to have her sick, demon processed **daughter healed**. The disciples asked Christ to send her away, and He made it very clear to her that he was sent only *"to the **lost sheep** of the house of **Israel.**"* (Matt. 15:24). Then the Lord chastened her further by bluntly telling her that it was not good that He take **"the children's (Jew's) bread** and throw it **to little dogs"** (Gentiles). But she was undeterred from her mission. Her reply, this undeserving puppy so to speak, was that she would **gladly accept whatever crumb** *"falls from the Master's table."* Her words will ring through eternity. What faith! What humility. As the **Bible records** it, she had captured the **heart of God** and her daughter was healed from that moment.

That is what this chapter is all about. Assorted and miscellaneous "crumbs" in the form of **quotes, Bible truths and lessons for life** will hopefully stir your soul or light your light.

So, **look around** under the Lord's Table, and perhaps you will find **some morsels** to keep and savor.

To All You Doubting Thomases

Every one of us in our Christian walk has **suffered** a time of doubt. However, when it comes **to God's Word:**

*"Believe your **beliefs** and doubt your **doubts**, but **never** doubt your beliefs or **believe** your doubts."*   Unknown

Amen

I have **no idea** where **this great quote** came from but I know I liked it and used it **at Easter.**

*"**The resurrection** is the Father's "**Amen**" to our Lord's cry, "It is finished!"*

The History Channel

Anyone **who doesn't think** God is in control of this old planet **hasn't read his Bible**.

From creation to Revelation, God has **already seen the story** from beginning to end, as if it were on a gigantic flat-screen TV. Nothing **is left to say,** except:

*"What **is history** but God's **unfolding of Himself?**"*
Unknown

Little Things of Life

If you have worked and struggled on the pathways of this planet, you know that the following is true in **your life** or the **life of your church.**

*"Little **is much** if God is in it, but **much is nothing** if God is not in it."*   Unknown

When Jesus Comes Again

Those of us who **look for the rapture** of the saints and the **coming of the Lord Jesus,** this little thought should warm your heart:

"There will be **a sound** *to hear,* **a sight** *to see,* **a miracle** *to feel,* **a meeting** *to enjoy, and a* **comfort** *to experience."*

Unknown

Working Too Hard for the Lord?

If you are busy **doing the Lord's work** and sometimes feel like you want to **walk away** from it all and let **someone else** carry the load for a while, listen to this:

"It is **better** *to* **burn out** *for Christ than* **rust out** *doing nothing."*

Unknown

Living in Corinth

Paul tells us much about the **lifestyle** of the citizens of Corinth, that ungodly **port city** of **sin and idolatry.**

Have **you** ever "lived" in Corinth? **I have,** and I am **not proud** of it. You probably **get my drift,** and I'm happy to say that I left Corinth **long ago,** but I remember the lessons I learned so that I can honestly feel for those who may stumble. My point, Christian, is that over the years I've witnessed this situation:

There are some **preachers and deacons** *who* **have never lived in Corinth,** *yet they are ready* **to trample underfoot anyone** *who foolishly takes a* **wrong turn** *and winds up there, no matter what the circumstances. I've seen it personally; no* **mercy,** *no* **compassion,** *and no* **forgiveness**—*and that, my brothers and sisters, is dead wrong.*

The Evil and Wicked

When we **read the news** and see what man is **capable of doing** to his fellow man, it makes one sick. When the full **depravity** of the human mind is exposed, one has to wonder why these people should even **share** the same air we breathe.

True, **judgment** is coming, but **Ezekiel 18:32** reminds us that God takes *"No pleasure in the death of the wicked."* Remember, **though wayward,** they are **still His children.**

The Trinity in One Verse

The longer I am a Christian, the more I **appreciate** the contributions of the Apostle **Paul,** that amazing man of God.

As an example, look at **2ⁿᵈ Thess. 3:5,** and a wonderful **Pauline example** of the power of **the Trinity:**

> *"Now may **the Lord (Holy Spirit)** direct your hearts into the love **of God (the Father)** and into the patience **of Christ (the Son).***

A Test for Truth

There are lots of **"new"** thoughts and ideas being **tossed around** in the churches today. I believe we should **test everything** by "what do **the scriptures** say?"

That great old preacher **Dr. Harry Ironside** said, *"If it's **new,** it's not true, and if it's **true,** it's not new."*

Empty Hands

We have become **a generation** of seekers of **"things."** There is a saying, usually **among men,** that goes like this; "He who has **the most "toys"** at the end, **wins."**

But **the truth** of the matter is that there are **three** times in life when we will have completely empty **hands:**

1. At **birth.**
2. When we **come to Jesus.**
3. At **death.**

Someone said, *"We brought **nothing** into this world and it is certain that we will **take nothing out."***

Life Values

If ever there was **a time** when people watched the **stock markets** or their **bank accounts** it is now. But we must keep all things in perspective, so take a look at Luke16:1–13 and think **on this:**

*"The value of money is **uncertain and temporary,** the value of **spiritual realities** is fixed and eternal."* **Unknown**

The Sickness of Revenge

Here is a thought that can be connected to the **Book of Esther** and the **plot of Haman** to destroy the Jews:

*"A man that **studies revenge** keeps his own wounds green, which otherwise would **heal** and do well."*   ***Francis Bacon***

Givers and Takers

I think most of you **already know** that the world is full of **two kinds** of people: **the givers** and the **takers.** Here's the difference:

*"The takers **eat well,** but the givers **sleep well.** "* **Unknown**

The Great Salt Crescent

I was on a tour boat on **Lake Seneca at Watkins Glen, New York** several years ago and I noticed that **U. S. Salt Company** has several large plants that border the lake. I asked **the captain** of the boat about them and **he told me this:**

There is a **massive crescent shaped band of salt** that is several thousand feet **under the earth,** some **so pure** it can be mined and then directly used for **medical purposes.** That band stretches **from** mid-west New York State, under Lake Ontario, into Canada, back down under Lake Huron, **and ends** near Detroit, Michigan. I was told that there is **still** enough left to **supply all of the world's needs for another 600 years!**

I asked him, **how** did it get there? "Dried sea bed," is what **the captain said,** but I think I have a **better explanation,** *"It is the glory of God to conceal a matter..."* **Prov. 25:2.**

It is **my firm conviction** that all the oil, water, minerals, precious stones, etc., whatever man would ever **need,** God put there **in the beginning.**

Our Forerunner

The writer of Hebrews, wrote in Hebrews 6:20 about Jesus, our **"Forerunner."**

What did that mean? Here is a **beautiful analogy** by **Mr. Anderson-Berry:**

> *"He **entered into,** so to speak, the **Holy of Holies,** so that **where He is,** we shall be also. He announced **our future arrival,** took **possession** of heaven's glories on **our behalf,** and has gone **ahead** to welcome His people and **present them** before the **Majesty of Heaven."***

Hope is Essential

From the **Book of Ezekiel,** written when the **Jews were in captivity,** comes the context of this thought of them having the **hope** of returning someday to their land:

> *"What **oxygen** is to the lungs, **such is hope** to the meaning of life."*   ***Emil Brunner***

Handling Disappointments

David was very disappointed that **his son Solomon,** not him, would be **the one** to build the Temple on **Mt. Moriah.** However, this **did not stop him** from continuing **to serve God.**

That was **the thought** behind this quote from **A. T. Pierson:** *"**Disappointments** are His **appointments."***

Christian Maturity

Warren Wiersbe made this wise observation:

*"**Maturity** doesn't come easily. There can be **no growth** without **challenges** and there can be no challenges **without change**. So, if our **circumstances never changed**, everything would be **predictable,** and the more predictable, the **less challenges life presents.**"*

Christians should know that this **has to do** with our spiritual walk. **1 John 1:5-10** speaks about **our walk in the light.** This allows us **to see** what is going on. That leads to **maturity, growth, and changes** for the better.

Wisdom and Knowledge

In the **Book of Job, Chapter 28,** Job notes how men **will dig and tunnel** deep into the earth to seek **precious jewels and gold,** risking their very lives. Why then will men and women not **"mine" and "dig"** into God's Word just as hard for **wisdom and knowledge?**

Spurgeon said, *"**Wisdom** is the **right use** of knowledge. **Just to know** something is not to be wise **because many know a great deal** but are **only greater fools** for it. There is **no fool** as great as the **knowing fool**. But to know **how** to use knowledge is to **have wisdom.**"*

Trials and Blessings

More from **Spurgeon**, writing about **the trials** of the Hebrews in **Exodus Chapter 18**:

> *"God's people are prone to engrave their **trials in marble** and their **blessings in the sand.**"*

God's Timetable

When the Hebrews finally **reached** the Promised Land, Moses had to explain to the people that the **conquest of Canaan** would still take time. That gave **Warren Wiersbe** cause to write this thought:

> *"**Obeying the Lord** means doing the right **thing** in the right **way** at the right **time** for the right **reason,** which is **to glorify God.**"*

The God of the Quail

God's **leading** and **providing** daily was evident in the lives of His children **during the Exodus**. The **cloud, fire pillar, manna, clothes not wearing out**–you name it; **He did it.**

But many of the **people's hearts** were still in Egypt and when they **cried for meat**, God sent quail by the tens of thousands. **Instead of thanksgiving**, they showed only **greed** and **hoarded** and devoured the meat **until they were literally sick**. God, in His wrath, allowed many to die because the meat had **spoiled** due of their lust and disobedience. All too soon, they had forgotten **Commandment #10:** *"**Thou shall not covet.**"*

It Pays to Listen

Let me share a short story about **getting your facts straight.** **Pat and I** were visiting some good friends in Idaho, **Jim and Helen Chase.** It was a Saturday and the girls went **"garaging"** while Jim and I did a few chores around the house. Preparing dinner that night, **Helen** said to me, "I saw a book today all about **mashed potatoes."** **"Mashed potatoes!?"** I said, **"How much** can someone write about mashed potatoes?" Helen looked at me, **laughed** and said, **"I didn't say** mashed potatoes… I said **Max Lucado!"**

How Do You Handle A Crisis?

Here are **3 quick thoughts** that I discovered about handling **a crisis** in life:

1. *A crisis isn't what **makes a person,** a crisis shows what a person **is made of.***
2. *What life **does to you** depends on what life **finds in you.***
3. *The **same sun** that **hardens** the clay **melts** the ice.*

With **some people,** a crisis is as simple as **a missed appointment.** Don't be **one of them.**

What Does God Hate?

Many of the **religious weak-kneed** find it impossible to believe that God would **hate anything.** To them, He is **only about love,** which is contrary to what the **Bible teaches.**

For instance, **in Psalms 5:4-6,** David makes it quite **clear** that God hates *"**workers of iniquity,** those who **speak falsehoods,** and **bloodthirsty and deceitful men."***

But, here is **the difference:** *His hatred **isn't emotional,** it's **judicial,** an expression **of His holiness.***

Son of Adam or Son of Christ

The **doctrine of election** lets God be God. He is **sovereign,** that is, He can **do as He pleases,** though **He never pleases** to do anything unjust.

Then, there **is man** and the **doctrine of free choice.** Man can do **as he pleases,** but that is where the similarity ends. So, we conclude:

"If left alone, all men would be lost. Everyone in this world is either "in Adam" or "in Christ." **Unknown**

Christ's Love for the Church

Paul, writing about the church in the Book of Esphesians said, *"Husbands, love your wives, just **as Christ loved the church**, and gave himself for her."* (Eph. 5:25) How does that apply to us individually? Here are three **key** points:

*1. In the **past**, Christ's love was manifested in **our redemption**.*

*2. In the **present**, it is seen in our **sanctification**.*

*3. In the **future**, it will be seen in our **glorification**.*

Unknown

Choice or Election

It amazes me sometimes how good **godly Christians** can get all worked up about **the doctrines** of **free will** or **predestination.** Quite frankly, **I believe in both** because I believe that **the Bible teaches both.** Want some proof? Listen–

The **same Bible** that says, *"**Elect** according to the foreknowledge of God," (1 Peter 1:2) also says, "**Whoever calls** upon the name of the Lord **shall be saved."***
Romans 10:13

Making or Mending

Paul had a great **burden** for all of his churches, especially **as a Pastor.**

Someone put it this way, *"**Church making** is heartbreaking, but **Church mending** is never ending."*

Bible Study 101

A good **thought** to **add** to your prayer **before** you study God's Word:

*"May my eyes **see** it, my mind **read** it, and my heart **retain** it."*

Comparing Mountains

There were **two mountains** in the area of **Samaria, Israel** that Old Testament Jews would use to remind themselves about **their choice** of either **blessings or curses.**

The Levite **priests** would gather on one side of one mountain, **the people** on the other mountain, and they would **sing back and forth. Mt. Gerizim** was the mount **of blessing** and **Mt. Ebal** was the mount **of curses or chastening.**

Spiritually, Christians live between two mountains: **Mt. Calvary** where **Jesus died for our sins,** and **The Mount of Olives** to which someday **He will return. Connecting the two** times together: *"God's **dispensations** change, but **His principals** never change. He blesses when we **obey** and **chastens** when we disobey."*   **Unknown**

Free Will and God's Purpose

Here's one you may **have trouble** getting your head around. I did...

Think about the many **circumstances and hardships** during the journey of the children of Israel **out of Egypt** to yet a new covenant with God when they went **into Canaan,** their new Promised Land:

> *"God's **sovereignty** doesn't destroy human **individuality or responsibility**. God is so great that He can **will us** to our freedom **to choose** but He will still **accomplish His purposes**."* **Unknown**

The Eyes of the Lord

Here's **a great thought** to start your day: as redeemed sinners, when we are in God's **will,** doing God's **work,** we are capable of feeling God's pleasure. **A. W. Tozer** made this beautiful observation in his book, **The Pursuit of God:**

> *"It is written that **the eyes of the Lord** run to and fro throughout **all the earth**. When the **eyes of the soul searching Christian** look **out** and meet the eyes of God looking **in,** heaven has **begun** right here **on earth**."*

The Great Discipleship Challenge

Luke Chapter 14 has many examples of what is **required of men** to be **full** and **complete** followers of the Lord. Jesus talks to His disciples at length and then finishes his parables with His oft used phrase, *"He who has ears to hear, let him hear"* *(Luke 14:35).*

Jesus starts the lessons with the details of **a great free supper.** He then tells the great multitude that followed **what kind of true disciple** He truly desired. His teaching was a great **combination** of **wooing** them to Himself and then **winnowing** them to **His purpose.**

Henry Drummond made this observation, *"The **entrance fee** into the kingdom of heaven is **nothing;** the **annual subscription** is everything."*

A Good Way to End–God Knows Me!

My wife, **Pat, found this** and suggested it could **be my final entry,** and I agree. The words in this final selection **refer to "me",** but wherever you read that something **refers to me,** insert **your own name,** and it will be **yours** too.

*"What matters, in the **last analysis** is that God knows _____ (add your name **here**). I am graven on the **palms** of His hands. **I** am **never** out of His mind. All **my** knowledge of Him depends on His sustained initiative in knowing _____. **I** know Him because He first knew _____, and continues to know _____. He knows _____ as a friend, one who loves _____, and there is no moment when His eyes are off _____, or His attention distracted from _____, and no moment, therefore, when His care falters.*

*It is to our **eternal blessing** that we know God, but how can we **ever get used** to the idea that **He knows us."***

J. I. Parker

PERSONAL REFLECTION

A Defining Moment–
Face to Face with Evil

As a citizen of **this world,** hopefully you understand that there is a **spiritual battle** between good and evil. **Jesus talked about it** and often **directly interceded** against evil spirits and demons. **Paul** also was under constant danger from **the devil's crowd.** If you read any newspaper today, there will be **stories of atrocities** committed by men that have to be demon driven.

I have a **defining moment** on this topic. For many years, I conducted a **weekly Bible Study** at a local assisted living and rehab facility. One of the nurses, a Christian lady named **Maria** sometimes asked me to **stop and visit a patient** who was very ill to pray with or for them. I was always happy to do so.

One day, she stopped me and asked if I would stop and see **Mr. Smith** (not his real name) in room #134, because he was **"not well at all."** That usually was her way of telling me that he was **close to death.** I said I would **gladly stop** after class.

When I entered Mr. Smith's room I was **not** shocked by what I saw because I had **seen it before.** Here was **a shell** of a man, **skin and bones,** curled up on his bed in the **fetal** position, eyes **closed,** and laboring **for each breath.**

I pulled a chair over **to the bed** and leaned down so he could **hear me**. "Hello Mr. Smith," I said, "Maria asked me to **stop by and visit**. I was wondering if I might **pray for you**".

At that point, instantly, his eyes **opened wide** and he turned his face upward so that he could **see me clearly**. From under **his right side** he pulled out **his arm and his hand** was curled into **a fist**. He **never said a word**, but looked me **squarely** in the eyes and seemed about to **punch** me in **the face** with whatever strength **he had left**. **What I saw** in those eyes was the **look of evil** and **what I felt** was Satan saying **"Get away** from him, **he's mine!"**

Immediately, I put **my hands up** and backed **away** from the bed saying, **"Hold on** sir, I didn't come to **upset you**, I was only responding to a request to stop **and see you**. I am leaving." I felt those **eyes of death** watching me all the way **out the door**.

It was an **upsetting experience**. Never before in visiting the sick had I felt as **helpless, unwanted**, and quite frankly, **frightened**. It was **a real experience** with **a real person** in the clutches of the devil. Satan **was not about** to give him up, to **me** or to **anyone else**.

PART FIVE
Final Thoughts

HOW DOES ONE DESCRIBE A CHRISTIAN?

We are living **in strange times,** especially for those who, without apology, call themselves **followers** of Jesus Christ, aka "Christians." As mentioned many times in this book, those of us who **call America home** are very fortunate to have the many freedoms we enjoy. **The world,** however, seems to be gaining more ground every day trying **to eliminate** the Christian voice concerning **morals, society, and values.**

Why is that? What do they **not** see or understand about us? What makes us **different?** Those are not hard questions for the true **believer** to answer, but even within our own ranks and community, we are **all different**. Consequently, when I stumbled across the following quote I had to make it **a part** of my **"Thought for Today."**

"A real Christian is an **odd** number anyway. He feels **supreme love** for One whom he has **never** seen, **talks** familiarly every day to Someone he **cannot see**, expects to go to heaven on the **virtue of another,** empties himself in order to be **full,** admits he is **wrong** so he can be declared **right,** goes **down** in order to get **up**, is **strongest** when he is **weakest, richest** when he is **poorest** and **happiest** when he feels **worst.** He **dies** so he can **live, forsakes** in order to **have, gives** away so he can **keep,** sees the **invisible,** hears the **inaudible** and **knows** that which passes as **knowledge.** And all the while, he may be confounding his **critics** by his unbelievable practicality: his **farm** may be the most productive, his **business** the best managed and his **mechanical skill** the sharpest of anyone in his neighborhood.

The man who has met God is **not looking** for something– he has **found** it; he is **not searching** for light–upon him the Light has **already shined.**

We have **not** here described a **superior saint**–merely a **true Christian,** far from **perfect** and with much yet **to learn;** but his firsthand acquaintance **with God** saves him from the **nervous scramble** in which the world is engaged and which is **popularly touted as progress."**

A.W. Tozer

HOW DOES ONE
BECOME A CHRISTIAN?

The Plan of Salvation

The Bible contains many verses pertaining to the **nations** of the world, **groups and peoples,** and **families and followers.** When it comes to the important step of **knowing God personally** in your heart, it must be on **an individual decision.** God has created a plan, **a path,** which one can follow to **meet Christ one on one** in order to be **saved** from the **judgment** the Bible says is sure to come.

This plan consists of **four steps.** Your part is: **you** must be open to the fact that the Bible is **God's Word,** that His message is **true,** and that your heart must be **open** to receive His message. Here are the steps:

1. **Acknowledge that you are a sinner.** Paul, writing to the Romans said in verse 3:23, *"for **all have sinned** and fall short of the glory of God."* **All** would include **you and me.** So that makes us **enemies of God.** How can **we change that?**

2. **Repent of your sinful nature.** Peter, preaching to the lost in Jerusalem, said, ***"Repent,** therefore, and **be converted,** that your sins may be blotted out."* Acts 3:19. We cannot **approach a holy God** without being **sorry for our sins.** This is what **repentance is all about,** and something you **must do.**

3. **Believe that God has already opened a way for you.** Jesus, Himself, said in **John 3:16:** *"For God so **loved** the world that **He gave** His only begotten Son, that **whoever believes** in Him should **not perish,** but have **everlasting life."** That **"whoever"** He mentioned **is you.** This part is **your choice.** Do you **believe** Christ?

4. **Now, your turn to confess and decide.** If you **do believe** what Jesus said and desire to **be one of His own,** pray right now for Him to **enter** your heart and **be your Savior.** What will this mean? Listen: in **Romans 10:9,** Paul wrote, *"That if you **confess** with your mouth the Lord Jesus and **believe in your heart** that God has raised Him from the dead, **you will be saved."** Friend, **would God lie?** Of course not, so make that important decision **now.**

If you have **trusted the Lord** and taken these steps with an open heart, **congratulations!** You have just **made the most important decision of your life.** Now, follow **God's plan for your life,** starting by **reading His Word every day.** You will be amazed how things will **appear new** and **different** in **your new found faith** and even the thoughts and comments in this book will make more sense as you read them. **God bless,** and walk with Him **every day!**

ACKNOWLEDGEMENTS

First of all, many thanks to **my wife, Pat.** She encouraged, corrected, and even added to the book content with several references.

To the **first readers** who waded through the original draft and commented on the content. That was a big help. Thank you **Arky and Shirley Nelson, Ray and Janice Williams, Frank and Leila Clymer, Helen Chase, and Darryl and Marie Williams**. I so appreciated all your suggestions, comments, and corrections.

THE FOLLOWING REFERENCES WERE USED:

- *Believers Bible Commentary of the Old and New Testaments,* Wm. MacDonald, Thomas Nelson Publishers

- *The Wiersbe Bible Commentary,* separate books of the Old and New Testaments, Warren Wiersbe, David Cook Publishers

- *Swindoll's Ultimate Book of Illustrations and Quotes,* Charles Swindoll, Thomas Nelson

- *The Darkness and the Dawn,* Charles Swindoll, Thomas Nelson

- *Matthew Henry Commentary,* Matthew Henry, Zondervan Publishing House

- *Works by or about A. W. Tozer* (23 in all) Wing Spread Publishers and Regal Publishers

- *The School of Biblical Evangelism,* Kirk Cameron and Ray Comfort, Bridge-Logas Publishers

- *1001 Quotes, Illustrations, and Humorous Stories,* Edward Rowell, Baker Books

- *1001 Unforgettable Quotes about God, Faith, and The Bible,* Ron Rhodes, Harvest House Publishers

- *Wise Words and Quotes,* Vern McLellon, Tyndale House Publishers

- *An Encyclopedia of Compelling Quotations,* R. Daniel Walkins, Hendrickson Publishers